For Peter,
in friendship
from Francis.
Oxford   May, 1985

COLLECTED POEMS 1960–1984

COLLECTED POEMS

1960–1984

FRANCIS WARNER

COLIN SMYTHE
Gerrards Cross, 1985

First published in 1985 by Colin Smythe Limited,
Gerrards Cross, Buckinghamshire

Distributed in North America by Humanities Press Inc.,
171 First Avenue, Atlantic Highlands, N.J.07716

British Library Cataloguing in Publication Data

Warner, Francis
Collected poems 1960–1984.
I. Title
821'.914   PR6073.A7238

ISBN 0–86140–206–5
ISBN 0–86140–207–3 signed ed.

Printed in Great Britain
Set by Grove Graphics, Tring, Hertfordshire,
and printed and bound by Billing & Sons Ltd.,
Worcester

Contents

5

EXPERIMENTAL SONNETS (1965)

MADRIGALS (1967)

LUCCA QUARTET (1975)

LYRICS, PUBLIC AND PRIVATE

from A CONCEPTION OF LOVE (1978)

from LIGHT SHADOWS (1979)

MORNING VESPERS (1980)

ENTR'ACTE

SPRING HARVEST (1981)

Note

Perennia was first published by The Golden Head Press, Cambridge, in 1962; the two shorter poems 'Fondling farewell' and 'I saw a shining lady' were also published by the same press, in the anthology *Garland*, in 1968.

Early Poems (1964), *Experimental Sonnets* (1965), and *Madrigals* (1967) were published by The Fortune Press, London. The American anthology *Poetry of Francis Warner* was published by Pilgrim Press, Boston, Mass., in 1970. *Lucca Quartet* (1975) was published by Omphalos Press, Knotting, Bedfordshire; *Morning Vespers* (1980) by Martin Booth, Knotting; *Spring Harvest* (1981) and *Epithalamium* (1984) by Martin Booth at Drayton, Somerset.

Maquettes: a trilogy of one-act plays (1972), *Lying Figures* (1972), *Meeting Ends* (1974), and *Killing Time* (1976) were all first published by Carcanet Press, now at Manchester. The complete sequence of six plays was republished, with an introduction by Tim Prentki, by Colin Smythe as *Requiem* (1980). *A Conception of Love* (1978), *Light Shadows* (1980), and *Moving Reflections* (1983) were all first published by Colin Smythe.

In the Contents pages of this book, the date given by each play is that of the play's first performance. The above are publication dates.

I give a tongue to my accustomed streets,
The buildings two slow rivers wind among;
Cambridge's sun-touched world of youth and song
That mellow Oxford's majesty completes.

For I have known them each day of the year,
Each paving slab and overarching bridge,
Each daffodil that yellow-peers its ridge
To wave at King's, or royalist-gentle Clare.

The bitterest wrench of winter's harshest claw
Experienced—graves dug with roadmen's drills,
Taking the pauper from his concrete floor,
Obese professor with religious frills.

For these two holy cities set apart
In meditation undeterred by time
Have been the shaping parents of my art,
Shown me their truth, and truth her paradigm:

Two market towns where scholars come to search
In bell-blest courts among old libraries
For secrets of the enzyme or the Church
Through paradoxical intricacies.

Here in St. Peter's, high among the spires,
With New Year's footfall crunching on the snow,
I pay a tribute of the debt I owe
Before my calendar of days expires.

Early Poems

LYRIC

Sweetheart lie still, that's not the sun
Touching the sky, dawn's not begun;
Sweetheart lie still, no night is passed
While we are tight like oysters clasped.

Darling, no daylight streaks the wall
Over our bodies, no birds call:
Ghosts of lovers unborn and dead
Shroud tomorrow from this bed.

Freshest bread needs freshest leaven,
Saplings will spring up anew;
Born we are in rain from heaven,
Rise again in morning dew.

LYRIC

There is no splendour in the sun
While you are absent from my arms,
And though I search till day is done
Remission in oblivion,
Watching the busy crowd go past,
Driving the brain, callousing palms,
No high philosophy rings true
Nor can contentment come, till you
Bring peace of mind, and rest at last.

TWO THINGS

I do not know the way my life will go,
 Or whether hopes speak true;
Whether old age will be the after-glow
 Of spirit blazing through
  This cabinet of clay
  That final day:

Or whether, forced by threadbare circumstance,
 I'll stunt these inmost thoughts
In midnight sweat of mercenary glance—
 The scrawled reports
  On volumes new
  For rushed review.

Whether the armies and the kingcups fall,
 Or nests and daisies perish from this land,
Whether the owls or politicians call,
 Demand my hand,
  I know that I
  Must love, and die.

LYRIC

When the wild
Rose is snapped,
And the child
Caught and trapped,
When the hare
Is crushed in the road,
A mental snare
Starts to corrode.

Love is beyond
The worldly man.
Marriage bond
Of Pot and Pan
Is a pale
Mockery;
Lifelong stale
Lechery.

Death's a brave
Ranting shout
In an empty cave;
Life gutters out.
Limbs of an antelope
Stretched in the grass
Make us grope
For the mountain pass.

When the slender
Primrose shoot
Pushing tender
Underfoot
Makes the child
Leap in the womb;
Then undefiled
Will the wild rose bloom.

LIBRARY THOUGHT

I sit at an old desk, among old books
Within a garret—a low-ceilinged, dusty
Attic; and the breeze-blown sun outside
Scarcely bothers to search these little windows
Leaded in diamond shape, thick-smoked, with husks
Embedded in the glaze: but my attention
Drifts from my writing to that sudden buzzing,
A hectic fly that's climbing round the leads
Insulted by invisible blockade,
Infuriated; stamping all six feet
And grumbling at the unattending sun.

What perseverance! Up he goes again
A little hungrier, more tired now
But still determined: wife at home no doubt,
Waiting his manly strut, deep-throated buzz,
The busy hum of his acquaintances
As they sip gathered nectar of an evening
Setting the world to rights. The old and frailer
One by one failing to call at dusk
Around the tenement built of three straws
Under the thatch. These start to shade his thoughts.
He is but in the very stride of life—
He fail to return? Unthinkable.
(Could that time come? Absurd.) No. Tries again.
Pause for a rest. The children! Up, and leaves
The window, racing round the dusty shelves
And back; back to that one small piece of glass.

My angry, tiny friend; I feel the same,
Absent from her: I'll let you out again.

BYRON'S POOL

Beside a field of corn, this tangled wood
Wakens to life at dusk; the trees around
Rustle in the evening air, and welcome home
The rooks and crows, the nightjars, magpies, wrens,
Squirrels, and all the host of animals
That live among their branches and their roots.
Nothing is still: the whole wood breathes and feels;
A water-vole runs through the undergrowth
And drops in the stream; a noisy pigeon calls
His four-fold, clownish cry. Numberless insects
Swarm round my head; and where I sit, a stump
Hollow with damp and age holds giant fungus.
Green leaves lie all around rich with the scent
Of wet and evening—sycamore and beech,
Elder and lime. One tatter'd oak-leaf falls.
A hawthorn tree breaks its spiked reflection
In the swirling river, as it leans from the bank
And sways its twisted trunk.

                High overhead
Rustle of branches merges with the rush
Of water on the weir; and to the west
Streaks of fantastic sunset hover still
Over the cottages of Grantchester,
While by the church beyond the cornfield
The moon is full and low over the barns
That store the harness, sugar-beet, and grain.

Darkness grows, and still my ears are full
With multitudes of sounds. Slowly the smell

Of mist creeps from the fields. Two new-hatched owls
Call, and there comes a hedgehog scuffling twigs,
Oblivious of me and all around him.
On flows a swan, with cygnets like herself,
But brown; on, past the weir. Bats play in the air,
Moths flirt with the river; a fish dives up
For a gnat, and leaves circles of water rippling
Outwards and outwards till they fade in weeds.
Hollows and humps in the ground take on new shapes
And shadows. Night transfigures all the wood.
The feel of darker beasts that search for prey
Pervades. Beetles are still: the hedgehog's gone:
The swans have passed; and on the leaves above
Patters the sound of the first midnight rain.

CHRIST'S HOSPITAL REMEMBERED

for John Ind

I ran down paths that Shelley trod,
Explored each copse and climbed each hill
From Donkey Bridge to Selsey Bill,
Oblivious of the muddy sod.

Down Sharpenhurst and Shelley Wood
I tumbled when I should have stayed
On cricket fields where Blunden played,
On boundary lines where pedants stood.

Those afternoons I dozed in class
In chalky rooms with peeling paint,
I felt the window bring the faint
Distracting smell of new-mown grass.

Or on a winter afternoon
I'd watch the dark outside descend
And let my wandering thoughts pretend
They wove strange circles round the moon.

My one desire was to be free
To roam through every field and lane
With chosen friends—and, in again,
Make music and write poetry.

MIGRAINE

I heard a glowworm crying,
Losing its light;
Listened to an owl replying
In plummet flight;
Felt its struggle, dying
Out there in the night.

Pain is the interstitch
Of love and life,
Straining the mind to its pitch
Mad in the strife;
Splitting the patient's stitch
As he dies by the knife.

Beauty intensifies
Cruelty:
Never an animal dies
But delicacy
Throbs where the egg-shell lies,
Broken free.

Cork up the night
Throw it to sea
Give back my sight
Pain go from me!
Wind up the dark
Drag in the day
Fight back this stark
Agony.

Will this pain
Never cease?
Must I strain
In vain for peace
Till my brain
Split its crease?

Time's a whore,
Lingering slow
When more and more
We ache for her to go:
The distant shore
That never seems to grow.

Pulse and ebb
Less frequent now.
My arm is lead
Across my brow.

Morning blows
And the owl flies away;
The glowworm knows
Eternity.

FOR A CHILD

I saw a squirrel on a tree,
And he laughing said to me
'Funny human, tell me why
You are so afraid to die?'

'Little squirrel,' I replied,
'Many, many folk have died;
Yet not one's come back to me
Proving immortality.'

'Timid mortal,' said my friend,
'Do you think that death's the end?
Know the acorn, when it dies,
Doubts an oak-tree will arise:

' "How could such a mighty tree
Spring from nut so small as me?"
For the acorn does not know
Where it grew, or what will grow.

'If you cultivate your shell
And starve the kernel in its cell,
When the earth gives you her bed,
Your true part is maggoted.

'You are sleeping in this life
In a shadow world of strife;
Yet when the dream grows old and lame
You will wake to life again.'

'Thank you, gentle squirrel. I
Am no more afraid to die.'
And, not wanting to seem rude,
I threw him a nut in gratitude.

BANK HOLIDAY

Now in the quiet countryside is heard
The screech of motor-bike instead of bird,
And country paths evaporate in dust
Flung up with fumes belched in the drivers' lust
For speed, and demonstration of just how
Much faster they can move than horse or cow.
The chickens scurry from the quiet lane
And squawking hop to kitchen door again,
And pigs, disgruntled, plod back to their sty,
Put out at being poked by passers-by.
Even the sleepy mole, safe underground,
Is rudely waked by noisy hooters' sound,
And in the hedges sparrows on their eggs
Disturbed by paper-bags and bottle dregs.
From leafy bushes, badgers' quiet retreat,
Protrude two pairs of city lovers' feet;
And on the grass around on every side
The trippers' litter fans the countryside.

THE LOVE OF GOD

No priest, with sanctuary bell,
No rhetoric of demagogue,
No missionary infidel
Brings me to the love of God.

But a simpler state of mind,
Seeing less, perceives the truth:
A milkboy, whistling down the wind,
Theologically uncouth,

Knowing nothing of the strange
Orthodox uncertainties
That perplex the subtle brains
Of divine nonentities,

Innocent of party ties,
Weather-worried at the most,
Lives and loves and laughs, and dies
Welcomed by the Holy Ghost.

SONG

Within a moment's meeting
    Life is pure again,
The heather springs its greeting,
    Eyes sparkle with new rain,

The trees and hedgerows glisten
    And pulses race delight,
Our ears as quick to listen
    As frosty stars at night.

LYRIC

Cliffs and forest pass away,
Towers and palaces decay,
Soon we too will end our day
    In dust.

Brief the rose upon its stem,
Briefer still the snowflakes' den,
Briefest, sick desires of men
    Soon past.

Donkeys bray and cattle low,
Men and women come and go,
Much the same as long ago
    In heart;

Passionate in battle-fight,
Passionate on wedding-night,
Passionate, with little sight
    Or far.

Pacing round his dented globe
He spends himself in greedy probe
Of business, while beneath the robe
    Or gown,

Doctor's fur and mortar-board,
Housewife's scowl at ironing-board,
Workman's trouser-holding cord,
    There stirs

Something old yet fresh as dew,
Hidden thoughts that one or two
May be numbered with those few,
    Those blest

Who have long transcended time
Widowed oak or toppled lime—
Lovers who have kissed in rhyme
    Singing still

Of interlocking minds and knees,
Of transcendental memories,
Of soul-dissolving ecstasies;
    And you

Will be called the queen of joy
And evoked by ardent boy
Thrilling one no longer coy
    And filled

With thoughts of us, and lovers gone
The selfsame way, in rhyme and song
Oblivious of right and wrong,
    In love:

And he will murmur as they lie
And pull their softest blanket high
'As she was to that poet's eye,
    So you

Have all the virtues he could find;
Purity and fire combined
Overcoming heart and mind;
    And we

Too shall live within the gleam
Their poetry sheds on our dream,
That poet, and his gentle queen,
    His Jill.'

KINVARA

I shall go where the swan soars,
Where the wind and the rain are born,
Where the coral lies on the bed of the sea,
Where the badger hides from the storm.

I shall feel the blanket of mist
That sweeps the Atlantic shore;
The splash of cold spring water,
The tufts where the breakers roar.

I shall hear the cry of gulls
Far out over the sea;
Spray of the waves washing the rocks,
Wind in the high cliff tree.

I shall watch my footprints fill
As the tide seeps in the sand:
Watch the sun on the wide horizon
Set, from the darkening land.

I shall learn what the cormorant knows
When, far beyond our sight,
He finds the thrill of a leaf that blows
In a gust on a stormy night.

I shall be filled with rushing thoughts
As the salt wind cuts my hair,
Filled with a boundless, lonely joy,
And find my haven there.

CANDLESMOKE

The friends I love are in my mind tonight;
Their images form in the candlesmoke.
Hiro, the Buddhist Muses' acolyte
Soft as a wine-dark tulip streaked with black,
Calm in kimono's ceremonial cloak
Listens to Henn who, spending his last breath
Studying eccentricities of death,
Conjures up visions from the bygone age
Of Ireland's greatness. C. S. Lewis—Jack—
Bunyan, Bacchus and Swift distilled in one—
And Davie, with glittering mind of bluest steel,
Fade in the smoke as Georgie Fraser's face
Bubbling over with amiability
Thickens and passes, giving final place
To purest poet of this company,
Priestess of ecstasy and natural pain:
The lonely sea-bird cries in Kathleen Raine.

Sligo, 1961

CASTLE LESLIE

My eyes are full, and I can see no more.
These sloping lawns, sweeping to the lake,
That rowing-boat that laps against the shore;
The walks, the cedars, chestnut trees that turn
From green to golden-russet, turn and burn
Out of the sunrise, deep into my soul
Until, filled with tranquillity, they make
This courtesy of nature mist the whole.

Gently the morning rain falls on the water
Tuning the whole to some mysterious key,
While merrily carefree dances Anita's daughter
Down to her pony, shaking her hair in laughter.
One day all this will seem a dream to her
When, grown into a bride, she hides no truth
From nature, but in happy ecstasy
Builds her life-love from memories of youth.

How shall I, in a busy London street
Walking amongst the traffic and flashing lights
And all the worrying hustle that will greet
Me when I leave, how shall I re-create
This healing peacefulness and natural state
Of mind, that breathes so seldom in the swirl
Of mercenary rush, and garish sights?
How there evoke this lake and laughing girl?

The soul must store its riches; feed upon
Moments of love and quiet such as these;
Mould them into one image: mine a swan
Floating upon the lake in this soft breeze;
And as the morning sun streams through the trees
Upon a swan, wherever I may be,
All will come back; the laughter, lake, the rain,
This overflowing, peace-grown memory.

The shadow moves on the wall. Ambivalence
Of image. Sun, or moving finger? Still
It moves in meditative patience—
A concrete myth; intangible, yet real
As knocker on a door, or hammered nail.
Why does it move so inexorably?
As though it knows all that mankind can feel,
And knowing, does not pause; but each detail
Of our existence reckons up, absorbs
Into itself; and still moves on; the weight
Of Calvary and of Hiroshima
And all the killing that makes up the freight
Of human history. Unshaped, and silent,
Still persevering on across the wall;
Neither a thing, nor god, nor animal:
Just a petitioner for penitence.

LYRIC

Time passes,
Youth flies away;
The greenest grasses
Soon are hay.

That bunch of straw
Is last year's nest,
And woodworms gnaw
The lavender chest.

Her eyes were brown,
Her lips were soft,
Her cheeks like down
The dew has washed.

We laughed and played
And loved our fill:
Till dusk we stayed
On Madingley Hill.

An acorn grows;
Is felled at last.
The west wind blows,
And the hill stands fast.

THE ESCAPE OF PRINCESS MARY TUDOR

King Edward on his death-bed lay,
　His young eyes dim and chill:
'Lord, save my Sister. This I pray,
　Preserve us all from ill.'

The boy king died; but word was sent
　By false Northumberland:
'Come, Mary, ere his life be spent
　And kiss his dying hand.

Speed, Mary! Turn your horse again,
　By all must you be seen.'
Meanwhile in London, Lady Jane
　Is nominated Queen.

At Hunsdon town, not far from Ware,
　The Princess heard his tale,
And taking five brave men with her
　Rode through the wind and hail.

But good Throckmorton sends a man;
　At Hoddesdon bridge they meet:
'Your Brother's dead! 'Tis the Duke's plan
　To weave your winding-sheet.

Northumberland has just proclaimed
　The Lady Jane as Queen.
He is no friend, his love is feigned;
　Spies on the road are seen!'

The Princess turned her faithful band,
　Northward she made her flight.
Across the tracks and meadow-land
　They rode into the night.

'Great Queen, grace us to be our guest',
  Cried Andrew, fair and tall.
'My cousin offers food and rest
  Yonder, at Sawston Hall.'

Weary, weary was the Queen,
  And weary were they all.
The hearths were warm, the stables clean,
  Tapestries hung the wall.

Gladly they rode into its light
  And gladly ate their fill,
Praying with thankful hearts that night
  That God would work His will.

As dawn was breaking, after Mass,
  Ere scarce the cocks had crowed,
The Queen dressed as a dairy-lass
  And behind her host she rode,

Past Two Pond Grove across the moat,
  Through Lady's Wash and on;
The Queen dressed in a milkmaid's coat
  Behind John Huddleston.

Through Hayfield Planten and Pampisford Wood
  To Pampisford Hill they came;
And when they looked back from where they stood,
  Sawston Hall was aflame.

'Then let it burn!' she cried. 'When gone,
  Timbers, roof and all,
We'll build another from the stone
  Of Cambridge Castle Wall!'

John Huddleston was knighted;
  His stone hall stands there still:
And where the Queen alighted
  Gorse grows on Pampisford Hill.

MY PATIENT PEN

My patient pen, help me in this,
Shape out these thoughts that break my bliss
In brine, make words to woo her heart;
Be courtier for her angry kiss:
Do this for me; I have no art.

For all my skills in rhyme are numb,
These tears have paralysed all dumb;
She rates them insubstantial, vain,
Having no faith in times to come:
My silent pen, win her again.

But what are words when faith is fled?
And what is truth when trust is dead?
Is there an art to recreate
Such joy, when cruel words are said?
Unkernel tenderness from hate.

And do not write your lines in ink,
Nor in this salt that makes me blink,
But use my blood; yes, take my all,
My eyesight, if it make her think
And know my heart is at her call.

Blood, sight and heartbreak, pain and fear,
My pen, say nothing is too dear,
Although she mock with curt retort.
What can I do to make her care?
The cry of every bird that's caught.

The sparrow snared by laughing boys,
The fledgeling caged for children's toys,
The eagle trapped in hunter's net,
The shrike, that smaller birds destroys,
Each seeks compassion in regret.

The nodding mole warm underground,
The nested finch and kennelled hound,
The tusky boar strawed in his sty,
Each seeks for hope where fear is found,
Each needs such love; and so do I.

Tell her, brave pen, although she say
Her path must weave another way,
Tell her no other way's for me;
In frost at night or mist by day
My harbour, my life-breath is she.

Come, gentle pen, help me in this,
Shape out these thoughts that break my bliss
In brine, call up your finest art;
Be courier for her angry kiss
And medicine my murdered heart.

THE CHALLENGE

I know this poetry of mine
Is a burst of the heart hammered into rhyme.
My thoughts run wild; to keep them in
I must have iron discipline
To rule and curb them. Even so,
I am no Michaelangelo.
His sonnets played upon my heart
Forcing my schoolboy nib apart
In childish imitations
Of his gemlike creations:
Not wholly wasted, for in time
I learned to scan as well as rhyme.
But now I struggle with that hardest art:
Shaping world-weary words to hold my heart.

ANIMULAE

Little poems, little poems,
I love you because you sing songs of spring
When I am in the snow,
And because you speak for me
When I am inarticulate.
You sing of distant mountain-peaks
When I am in Tufnell Park,
And smile at things which
When I am in her presence I cannot say.

My little poems, who will ever read you?
Who will ever publish you?
Yet I love you, good and bad,
Because you tell of love and spring and tears
When I am too weary to tell of them myself.

LYRIC

A swallow skims the icy sedge
And settles on my window-ledge
To shake its feathers in a ball,
Warm itself, rest awhile; then fall.

A crocus waking in the grass
Picked as the merrymakers pass.
And is love, too, on such brief loan
It visits, buds, and turns to stone?

FRAGMENT

In these volcanic, seething days
Of enemies, uncertainty,
Deception, insincerity,
And turning twenty thousand ways

To grasp some foothold on this rock,
The drop below, vultures above,
One constant's certain as the clock;
Our mutual agony of love.

NEWS

First hint of life's end,
And eagle's muscled shelter over nest,
Leopard's tread, panther's paw,
Guiding whisker of wandering water-vole,
Swift eye of swallow flying South,
The sleepless, plunging, luminous tropical fish,
Are strange. Unrealized, unrecognized before;
Never before having understood
The gentle are not weak.
What is that icy hand on the base of my skull?

PRAYER

Fiercely burn, fiercely burn,
  Lonely Spirit of Light!
Make the plunging eagle turn,
Teach the broken man to earn,
Help the coward to return
  Back to the fight.

Set the weary artist free,
  Sailing alone
On the materialistic sea,
Battered by vulgarity,
Caverned in mortality:
  Sinew this bone.

Save our vision from decay,
  Undermined
By gentle ridicule each day,
And earthbound critics in the way
Stinging till it hurts to pray:
  Make us not blind!

Teach us truly how to hate,
  And to discern
How to prune and isolate
All our souls should nauseate.
Teach us always to create;
  And to learn.

THRESHOLD

A brutal trace across an adolescent sky,
  And boyhood's gone.
A slight, sophisticated touch of mockery,
  And where there shone
The eagerness, the trusting faith of youth,
The natural fearlessness and confidence
That every man when shown must love the truth—
This glowing optimism of ideals
Reels, and is snuffed by adult common-sense.

Those questions are not easy, cannot be
  Solved in a statement.
The fugue must weave greater complexity
Of new experience upon old themes of doubt, piling,
    till spent
In questionings the resolution comes,
Stating again, in deeper majesty,
Those hard-won bars afresh, while muffled drums
Approach to turn the page, and silence all the resonance
    of breath.

PERENNIA

for Mary

*Only by looking towards the Beyond as the true goal
of ecstasy can man become balanced in the present.
Balance depends on ecstasy.* *

I

I stretched and lay beside the stepping-stones
Down on the grass beneath a rowan tree,
And watched the sunlight's warm September tones
Tinge a contented, droning bumblebee
Who buzzed to where a wine-filled blackberry
Had rolled beneath a fallen cock of hay.
Colourful berries hung the hedge by me
Sparkling like daylight glowworms, small and gay;
Hawthorn and hips and haws danced in this sunshine day.

* Edgar Wind, *Pagan Mysteries in the Renaissance*
(London: Faber & Faber, 1958), p. 53.

45

II

The river idled in among the weeds,
Eddying round each obstacle that came,
And lulled the sycamore's slow-falling seeds
That fluttered down to make a teasing game
For hungry minnows, searching for a grain
Or water-fly. The clouds borne in the stream
Drank in the sunlight and threw back again
Flashes of warmth from where cool trout and bream
Slept while the liquid music murmured through their
    dream.

III

Soaring aloft in the windswept blue of the sky
Climbing and plunging over the humpbacked air,
Swallows swept and signalled their twittering cry
Over the sun-turned treetop branches where
The streambound dragonfly would never dare
Venture, but hides from his fork-tailed enemy,
Flashing his myriad colours through the clear
Ripples down to the fishes' sanctuary,
Far from the swallows' spontaneous trill of ecstasy.

IV

A steady wind went rustling through the trees
And swayed the beeches by the river brink,
Combing a cloud of gold and copper leaves
Across the sun, making it dance and blink,
Settling at last to float away, or sink.
And here, away from London and the lights,
I lay against this rowan tree to think
Of things remote from Piccadilly sights—
The Eros statue traffic and the throbbing nights.

V

Scent from the fields around, the rich, brown nuts
Under the chestnut trees, far barley sheaves
With pheasants stalking in the stubble ruts,
Dandelion seeds blown on the rustling breeze,
The clover buzzing with the busy bees,
Feel of the sheep-cropped grass beneath my palm,
The lapping of the water—all of these,
Soothing my mind like some old mystic charm,
Begged me unpack my flute to join their harmless balm.

VI

Then, as I played, gentle flute music came
From all the hill around in soft reply:
The breeze grew stiffer now, and drops of rain
Fell sprinkling from the cloud-flecked summer sky.
I piped more loudly, and the wind grew high,
Billowing blackened mountains through the air
Until the birds had all begun to fly
For shelter to the leafy squirrel's lair,
Showering ivy sprigs, which settled in my hair.

VII

I crouched and played yet more, and still the wind
Thickened and drove the falling leaves in whirls,
Racing them round and round till they were pinned
Beneath a stone or tree-trunk, or in furls
Were hurled to where the savage water curls
His waves against an elm log in the mud,
Banking the leaves in dams against the swirls
And torrents of the overflowing flood,
Pounding the wind and water's music through my blood.

VIII

My piping died away, and this rough storm
Suddenly sank to a breath like a song half sung,
Now scarcely stirring teazles with its warm
And whispering wind, dawdling its way among
The rain-filled hedges where the berries hung.
A startled spider dropped, bright wide awake;
But gazing past the twig to which he clung
I saw a woman by a small flood-lake
Weeping into the stream as if her heart would break.

IX

Her long hair hung about her childlike face
Framing it in a waterfall cascade
Of dew-drenched gold, giving a gentle grace
To all her form, down which the sunlight played
With flickering smiles while to the stream she prayed:
'Why has the cruel wind carried me here
Away, alone today when, had I stayed,
I should have been a bride? What did it fear?
Help me to understand, full stream, so calm and clear.'

X

The steady river ran without a pause,
But from an acorn hedge a cricket hopped
And, waiting for a while crouched on all fours,
He sprang into her hand as though he'd dropped
From nowhere. She, surprised and happy, stopped
Her tears, slowly turning her eyes to find
A near-by branch, and on the fork she propped
Her arm and waited. Then the cricket chimed,
'You have been worshipped more than may your
    humankind.

XI

'Wild animals and insects, brooks and birds,
Have listened for your name in every sound
And sung it through the air. The goats and herds
Of sheep and cows have sent your name around
The hills until they echoing rebound
With wafted paeans to your beauty, praised
Till all the natural orchestra is drowned
In echoes flooding back, and all are dazed,
Crying, "Perennia! Perennia!" amazed.

XII

'You have been carried by the wind, unseen,
And set away from cheering crowds apart;
For Hespera, the jealous Goddess Queen,
By you has lost her rule over Man's heart:
And she who smooths the oceans and can chart
The wandering planets' courses will not bear
One who will rival her, with power to start
Spring fires of love in mortals everywhere;
And harsh the punishment she cries on those who dare.

XIII

'But in this place, beside this wooded bank,
You will be safe awhile.' Then he was gone
Back to his hedge before she tried to thank
Her mentor: and, thinking herself alone,
She slipped the crumpled dresses she had on,
Standing reflected in the limpid pool;
And treading gently on a stepping-stone,
Fanned by the sun, she felt the water cool
Her feet while shoals of fishes swam by in a school.

XIV

Slowly she slipped her sunlit body in,
Parting the stream which strayed around her limbs
Washing her loosened hair and tender skin,
While she bathed as the lazy goldfish swims,
Or as the long-legged summer insect skims
The idle surface as he drinks his fill
From pools and shallows where the water brims
Its sides; so like a water-lily still
She turned and floated, soon forgetting all her ill.

XV

And cooled, refreshed and softened by the brook,
She climbed upon the bank and closed her eyes
To lie and feel the sun, or gazed to look
Up at the wisps of cloud and butterflies
Fluttering to and fro, while high birds' cries
Warn them that they must leave their happy play,
Brushing the dreamy heat-haze where she dries
Her slender body. So the sun's warm ray
Caressed her sleeping stream-washed figure where she lay

XVI

Soon down the winding, wooded hillside track
A boyish figure with a bow appeared
Searching into the sun, his head thrown back
Showing a face that wore as yet no beard,
Whose hair fell loose like sheep's wool newly sheared
Across his neck: he unsuspecting came
To where she lay asleep; and stopped, and peered,
Scarcely believing that her face and frame
Could be so beautiful and yet remain the same.

XVII

Entranced he gazed, his goatskin slung across
His body while he stood and wondered long
Whether this creature sleeping on the moss,
Warmed by the sun and lulled by insects' song,
Was mortal or a goddess, to belong
In such tranquil surroundings; if some freak
Of Nature had united weak with strong
To make perfection. Aching now to speak,
Yet fearful to disturb her rest, he kissed her cheek.

XVIII

As yet too young to know his archery,
His heart was filled with love of purest fire
And all his soaring spirits, once so free,
Were anchored now in innocent desire
To share with her the cheerful chaffinch choir
That sang above her head; to hear her laugh;
To trace safe paths across the dangerous mire,
Show her his mountain goats, his tender calf
New-born, his secret haunts, his new-cut hazel staff.

XIX

She felt the touch upon her cheek and saw
The boy-god's face a moment over her
So brilliant that she blinked; but saw no more,
For he had vanished without sound or stir
Seeing her eyes were mortal, that they were
Unable to look safely on a god.
But as he vanished a small tuft of fur
Fell from his goatskin where his hazel rod
Had rubbed. She took it, shaking off a sleepy nod.

XX

Heavy with rest she looked about again
And saw all as it was before she slept;
But now her breast filled with a yearning pain
To see the man whose image still she kept
Before her eyes, and mirrored teardrops crept
Down her smooth cheeks to fall into the tide.
But as she clasped the fur and softly wept
A robin hopped his way close by her side
And quizzically waited till her eyes were dried.

XXI

Then birds of all descriptions gathered round
At peace with one another—hedge-sparrows
And bunting, wrens and larks flew to the ground
Fearlessly mingling with the hawks and crows.
Ibis and lapwing spread their summer shows
Of multicoloured feathers, and with these
Peregrine falcons from far Iceland snows
And eagles from the golden Pyrenees
Settled upon a branch or circled round her knees.

XXII

And animals of many breeds and kinds,
Rabbits and does, foxes and water-voles,
Hedgehogs and donkeys, kingly stags and hinds,
Earthworms and beetles, blindly burrowing moles,
Pushed through their tunnels or crept from their holes,
Or travelled from thick forests and wide parks
To see her with their young—mares with their foals,
Goats bringing kids with strange, distinctive marks,
And sheepdogs guiding lambs and sheep with careful
    barks.

XXIII

Now all of nature seemed to hold its breath.
Not a leaf stirred. A moorhen's feathers brushed
A stone and paused. The air was quiet as death.
The river that awhile before had rushed
In torrents hesitated and was hushed.
No creature moved. An ivy-coloured oak
Older than all the forest, with trunks crushed
And torn by many a furious tempest, broke
The silence and at last to this great crowd he spoke.

XXIV

'Perennia will live amongst us, free
To make her peace here. Let her never lack
Shelter or food, clothing or company.
When she calls music, echoes will blow back
Your bird-songs from hill-hollows till they pack
The sunbeams full of sounds. When she needs food
Fetch her ripe nuts and let small squirrels crack
Them for her. Mice, bring hedge-wine newly brewed,
And birds of prey, protect her as your tender brood.

XXV

'These hill-slopes, lady, and this cave are yours,
Where every night Eros, unseen, will come
To be your close companion when the moors
And ditches shudder, when the kestrels shun
The treetops and the badger's feet are numb.
And, when the tender corn shoots in the stalk
And you are warmed by the fresh April sun,
Eros will laugh with you and share your talk
When after dew-filled days you make your homeward
    walk.

XXVI

'All here is yours, and though you may not see
His godlike body he will not be far.'
Then with these words the old, majestic tree
Ceased as the early, brightest evening star
Shone in the sky. The grey bat and nightjar
Rose from their perches. Softly, wave on wave,
They all departed without trace or scar
Left on the ground. She watched the last rook brave
The cool night air, then stood and peered into the cave.

XXVII

Flickering of ten thousand glowworm cells
Shadowed the floor and shone upon the walls,
And tiny sounds from comfrey and harebells
Mingled with music spun from waterfalls
That splashed the sides of inner rock-hewn halls
Where malachite and agate, amethyst,
Fluorspar and bluejohn, jades, opals,
Topaz and lapis lazuli were kissed
By wistful perfumes till her eyes were full of mist.

XXVIII

And then more lovely than a well-played lute
The voice of Eros spoke beside her ear
Telling her to go in and eat the fruit
That lay upon the table, and to cheer
Herself with honey-mead, the country beer;
And tell him all that she had felt that day;
To lie down on the bed of maiden-hair
And spend the hours in happiness and play
Of childish innocence while he beside her lay.

XXIX

When first light broke the boy-god sadly strayed
Into the forest while Perennia
Slept on the ferns within the cavern shade.
But on the farther shore now calling her
By name, the voice of salt Salacia,
Her elder sister, woke her from deep sleep
With calling through the misty morning air.
She wrapped a silk about her form to keep
It dry from dew and ran to where the willows weep.

XXX

'O strong West Wind, carry my sister here
As you did me', she begged. 'Set her beside
These willow trees. Warm her that we may cheer
And rest her well after the weary ride
In search of me; lift her across this tide!'
Obediently the West Wind took his load
And brought Salacia in one gust-stride
Across to where the folded daisies stowed
Away their secrets till the morning cocks had crowed.

XXXI

When she saw all the joy of this demesne,
The natural happiness this valley held,
Plenty and peace beyond all she had seen
In years of travel, then her heart rebelled
Till jealousy beneath her eyelids welled:
Yet she contrived to cover her disgrace
Probing with artful questions, which compelled
Her sister to describe the god and place,
And tell at last that she had only glimpsed his face.

XXXII

'Sweet sister,' soon she smiled, 'this luxury
Of animals and birds for retinue
May fascinate; but can your Eros be
So radiant that he must hide from you
In stealthy midnight visitings his true
Form? Can he be a pure, immortal child
Such as you say? If he is fine to view,
Why does he hide a body that is mild
And harmless? He may be a beast, gross and defiled.

XXXIII

'For many a satyr has an easy charm
And glowing look, insinuating trust
That merely leads us on to our own harm
Till we are prostituted to its lust
And every passionate and goatish gust
That shudders through its body. Though he fawns
And flatters you with presents, yet you must
Fly from this place before full morning dawns
And listen to the loving voice of one who warns.

XXXIV

'Or if you will not leave this haunted glade,
Tonight, when he is sleeping by your side,
Take up a glowing branch that you had laid
Upon the fire before the embers died,
And by its light destroy your sleeping guide
Before you are disfigured in your turn.'
The West Wind blew upon the roughening tide
Making the angry waters boil and churn
And carried back Salacia with buffets stern,

XXXV

And set her down. But she returning heard
Upon this farther bank a hidden sigh
That straying Eros heaved who, deeply stirred
Within his heart, wondered the reason why
His pulse beat restlessly and mouth seemed dry,
And all his sports and pleasures seemed to cloy
After his night spent in the cave near by
With pure Perennia. She guessed the boy
Who sighed unseen to be her sister's source of joy.

XXXVI

Gently she whispered, 'Young god, in distress
When all your kingdom loves to wake and sing—
What is it that disturbs your happiness?
Have you not, with my sister, everything
You could desire? Perhaps some hidden spring
Wells up within to trouble you, although
You cannot yet describe it. Does this bring
You sighing to this bank? If that is so
Come to your loved one's sister: learn what I will show.

XXXVII

'For you must lie by me and kiss me as
You did your own Perennia, and I
Will teach you secrets that the grown man has
But hides from childhood's uncorrupted eye;
And all your misery will pass you by
As golden daybreak floods your youthful heart.'
In unsuspecting ignorance of why
Salacia should scheme to make them part
He lay, though still unseen, to learn this lady's art.

XXXVIII

A mighty vision burst within her head
As mortal with immortal was combined.
She dreamed she saw a flying waggon led
By two great horses and controlled behind
By Eros tugging at the reins, confined
Within his chariot. The right-hand horse
Was white as snow and knew the driver's mind:
The black one plunged and reared up in its course
Dragging its driver down with devastating force.

XXXIX

Then blasted with milk of eternity
Her body scattered in a thunderflash
Over the hill-slopes far out to the sea;
And Eros, knowing all, fled with the crash
Back to Perennia lest she should dash
Terrified into danger: but the trees
Protected her; the river would not splash
Her where she sat, with mushrooms on her knees
Gathered while waiting for his absent melodies.

XL

Now loving her beyond all other things,
As he returned and found her sitting still
Upon the tree-stump near their cave, his wings
Grew weary, and he roamed with her until
The sun went down and she had played her fill
Among the hedges, searching every briar
For berries; then, when all the glade grew still
And owls flew low, she turning to retire
Within their cave lay down and rested by the fire.

XLI

Though he had learned the cause of his strange pain
The night before, he was content to lie
In innocence with her and to refrain
From any harm, afraid lest she should die
Delirious. He whispered songs to try
To soothe her tender body into sleep;
And to his softly spoken lullaby
She dozed upon the yielding fern-moss heap
As round the cave the shadows lengthened and grew deep.

XLII

In unmistrusting love and simple faith
Eros slept wrapped in darkness from all sight:
But in her dreams there hovered like a wraith
The figure of a satyr such as might
Haunt dying men on execution night.
She woke in horror and lay still as stone,
Watching the embers glow. Then, by their light,
She stretched to reach a branch that lay alone
Kindling within a cave-draught where the night had
    blown.

XLIII

She lifted up the brand in breathless stealth:
It faded low. She blew, and a bright spark
Flew like a comet showing all the wealth
And beauty of his body through the dark,
Falling to burn his shoulder with a mark
That seared into the skin. Then he was gone:
And she collapsed in sorrow for her stark
Betrayal of his love, and fell upon
Her lonely bed and wept until the daylight shone.

XLIV

Eros meanwhile, under his mother's care
Had been plucked back to heaven when the burn
Singed, and was held in close confinement there
Until entirely healed, for his stern
Mother determined he should not return
To earth again till her competitor
In beauty was destroyed. She watched him yearn
For her companionship and sought the more
To cauterize his love and pay her ancient score.

XLV

She meditated how the wind had seized
Perennia upon her wedding-day
At her command, and now, with thoughts diseased
By jealousy, she saw that while away
Her son had saved her victim; and their play
Of adolescent love had brought more true
Joy and contentment to this child of clay
Than ordinary mortals ever knew.
Then in her mind dreams of retaliation grew.

XLVI

Pondering on a strange and fitting task
To lay upon her, one that seemed beyond
All human power, she sent a dove to ask
Perennia to enter in a bond
Of friendship. In return she could respond
By searching all the river-bed to count
The hairs upon the lily-stalks. This fond,
Obedient dove flew earthwards to recount
Her message as the crescent moon began to mount.

XLVII

The falling moonbeams made the pebbles shine
White in the pools and shallows as she heard
The bitter task that Hespera in fine
And flattering phrases sent her by this bird.
She stared down where a water-spider stirred
Beneath the surface near his bubble trap,
Seeing her own reflection miniatured
Within his airy prison, while the lap
Of water seemed so pure she felt her mind would snap.

XLVIII

A newt disturbed a clump of meadow-sweet
And peered through clusters of marsh-marigold
To catch a caddis-fly. His weblike feet
Darted round crowfoot stems to find a hold,
Or paused among those loosestrife buds which fold
The purple flowers close within their leaves
To shield them from night vapours and the cold.
She watched him jerk and scamper by degrees
On to a full-lipped lily, where he seemed to freeze.

XLIX

She started up. Along the water's edge
Thousands of tiny creatures had appeared:
Lizards and newts crawled from the willow-sedge,
And daphnia and water-boatmen steered
Among the traces water-mites had cleared.
Fat bullfrogs made their way, with brook lamprey
And softest moths blown from the old-man's-beard
To settle on this lily carpetry,
While fishes searched the mud and depths they could
    not see.

L

Then, understanding that the friendliness
Of this grey, moonlit host united here
Was all to save her from the bitterness
Of Hespera, she cried away her fear
In sobs of joy; and when the newt drew near
Giving the answer that the Queen required
She sang her gratitude in tones so clear
It seemed the waterfalls had all conspired
To hold her love-filled melody when she retired.

LI

Hespera heard her answer, but in hate
Ordered a second task—that she should send
An apple plucked from where grey, desolate
Crags on the mountain towered to contend
With piling clouds; determined so to bend
This mortal's will, and break her in a test
Of such immensity, that in the end
Death would be prayed for as a welcome guest
Before the climbing sun had settled in the West.

LII

Waking within the lonely cavern mouth
Perennia saw gillyflowers blow
Beside the river. Then from out the South
A speck came flying, and she watched it grow
Until the dove flew down to let her know
Its message. With a torn, half-stifled cry
She let her tears of desperation flow,
Praying that distant Eros would be by
To give her his forgiveness if she was to die.

LIII

But from her side a golden eagle soared
Into the sun to find the fruit for her,
And circling where the precipices roared
Severed the apple for Perennia,
Flying in feathered bold regalia
Northwards again to lay it at her feet.
She sent the dove with this ambrosia
Back to its cruel mistress; and to greet
The mighty bird's return fed him raw flesh to eat.

LIV

The Queen of Beauty would not rest until
Her unoffending rival had been killed,
Or broken utterly beneath her will,
Ordering now the fire should be twice filled
With coals and branches till the cave was grilled
In heat unbearable, and all that night,
While natural life beneath the moon was stilled,
The child should stay within the furnace light
Locked in a blaze that made the metalled rocks unite.

LV

A thousand silkworms spun a thick cocoon
Over her body, and the phoenix came
To give her courage from his magic tune,
While ancient salamanders, blind and lame,
Give her their power to withstand the flame—
Secret for untold weary centuries.
She tremblingly endured the pain and shame
Through crawling hours that stretched eternities,
Till release came at last with morning's certainties.

LVI

The unrelenting goddess now designed
One hazard more for her to undergo:
She must descend into the grave to find
And bring back Beauty from the world below,
Beyond that stream where lethal waters flow,
Venturing to the kingdom of the shades.
No living mortal had been known to row
Across that river twice, and in those glades
Of chalk-like soil no nightingale's clear serenades

LVII

Disturbed the silent kingdom of the dead.
Perennia was stunned into a trance
Of horrified amazement. Through her head
Imaginary phantoms seemed to dance—
One leering with a gross, malicious glance,
Another gaping through an earth-filled skull
At her—and as she watched them grin and prance
She turned to die rather than try to cull
Trophies from lands where even gods grew pale and dull.

LVIII

Her gentle river, that had washed her heart
So many times with music of content,
Would surely understand, and take her part
While she dissolved her body, and prevent
The suffering that drowned souls underwent.
This river knew her thoughts and, with a stir
That hardly rippled, asked her to relent,
Taking upon the quest that piece of fur
That Eros, when he first appeared, had left with her.

LIX

Holding it in her hand she strayed that day
Where scythes and sickles had been left to rot
As though the reapers had been called away
Suddenly, leaving all within that spot
Carelessly unattended and forgot.
She gathered and arranged them round an elm
Which wreathed its twisted branches in a knot
That masked a gong, spreading to overwhelm
The entrance of a path to the infernal realm.

LX

With an unearthly courage she went on,
Coming to where a ferryboat was moored
Near to a landing-stage, its rudder gone.
She tore a piece of fur and stepped on board
Giving it to the guide who was restored
To thoughts of love and youth on touching it.
And when the journey on the bitter ford
Was passed, Perennia bestowed a bit
On every beast that blocked her entry to the pit.

LXI

At last she viewed the splendours of the grave,
The terrifying and majestic scene
Where all the souls of the departed wave
Rank upon rank, far as the eyes can glean
A glimmering of twilight. Here the Queen
Of Night sat high enthroned above the throng,
Knowing the mortal's errand, having seen
Her journey down, and followed it along
The labyrinthine paths beyond the midnight gong.

LXII

The Queen gave her a casket with the words
That it should not be opened. But when she
Returned, as she had come, to where sleek herds
Of cattle grazed beneath the wych-elm tree,
And saw again all nature's artistry,
She longed to take some beauty from the case
To win her Eros back again, that he
Loving her would forgive all her disgrace.
She opened it; and fell like death upon her face.

LXIII

The little mist of beauty had enclosed
Her vital spirits till she lay so cold
That all her living kingdom round supposed
Their mistress dead. Ravens and night-owls tolled
Their evensong, and sad marsh-marigold
Lowered their petalled heads to touch the brook,
While clouds across the sun seemed to enfold
The world in mourning till it made it look
As though the tears of life were in each leaf that shook.

LXIV

But Eros, now recovered from his burn,
Yearning to see Perennia once more
Watched for a moment when he might return
Unnoticed by his mother, to restore
The laughter that her eyes had held before
When both together they had mocked the rain,
Slept in the sun and run along the shore
Like young gazelles, untouched by hate or pain,
Resting only to wake to happiness again.

LXV

He came back to the stream—but all was changed.
No birds, no animals bathed in the sun.
Where herds of sheep and goats before had ranged
Browsing within the meadows, now not one
Appeared. The very fishes seemed to shun
The surface where the lily-leaves were spread
In rich profusion. Silence seemed to stun
His senses. Then, by where the elm-tree shed
Its leaves he saw his love lying as one struck dead.

LXVI

And yet no agony was in her face:
Beauty had calmed her brow in perfect peace.
The harshest sufferings had left no trace
Upon her cheeks, for sleep had brought release
From all her miseries, and made them cease.
Unutterable love surged in his heart
As, bending down, and taking off his fleece
To cover her, he saw her earthly part
Outshone the brightest miracle of heaven's art.

LXVII

He brushed away the mist with gentle breath;
Then, trembling in her eyes, she saw him stand
In all his radiance. The sleep of death,
The great descent into that other land
From which no man returns, the tasks, the brand,
Were over now. She gazed with steadfast eyes
Upon her love, who raised her by her hand.
The whole of nature burst to life with cries
Of rapture, and Perennia cried to the skies:

I have danced, with eternity dawning,
        lain between delicate petals of night,
Stroked the blue butterfly-wings of the morning,
        tiptoed the moon on a cobweb of light,
Washed in the waterfall, made my limbs moister,
        tickled a slippery trout by the gills,
Plunged with the otter and yawned with the oyster,
        ridden a stallion over the hills.

Ride on with me to the lands of tomorrow,
        sail where our souls will be sundered no more,
Far from where breakers of parting and sorrow
        pound on the heart like the waves on the shore.

I have run down the rainbow and covered my traces,
        blown on the wind and sung to the sea,
Whispered brave words in the holiest places
        setting the terrible glaciers free,
Taken the sting from the arrogant lightning,
        tied up a maniac murderer's hands,
Lain by the lizard to watch the day brightening,
        burned with the sun on the tropical sands.

Ride on with me to the lands of tomorrow,
        sail where our souls will be sundered no more,
Far from where breakers of parting and sorrow
        pound on the heart like the waves on the shore.

I have cradled the rabbit new-born in the burrow,
        fanned it with down from a kingfisher's crest,
Followed the field-mouse searching the furrow,
        pouching up grain to take back to her nest.
Come to a land where the roebucks are bounding,
        pick up a thistle and knock on the sky:
Dance to the fields where the huntsmen are sounding
        the horn of a dawn in which hatred shall die.

Ride on with me to the lands of tomorrow,
        sail where our souls will be sundered no more,
Burst through the bindings of passion and sorrow,
        ride on my heart like the waves on the shore.

And with her song still ringing in my ears,
I woke beside the Box Hill stepping-stones.
My flute had slipped among some travellers'-tears,
Where in the evening wind brown autumn cones
Dropped through the weeds and made wide, rippling
    zones.
A bonfire flamed and crackled cheerfully
Scenting the air with smoke, till in my bones
I knew that I had seen reality
Lying upon that bank beneath the rowan tree.

Cambridge, September 1961

A LEGEND'S CAROL

for Roger Martin

The air was purified with frost,
And many a lonely mariner lost
    Upon the sea
Raised a numb hand to shield his sight,
And stared up at the starry night
    In reverie;
While far away, in from the shore,
   Ice on the roadside wells
Thickened, and snowdrifts round each door
   Deadened the cattle bells.
        The sleeper shrank deeper
        And pulled his blankets high,
        While burrow and furrow
        Lay still beneath the sky.

A crowd of drunken revellers
Laughed at a pair of travellers
    Who called for room.
They mocked the man for his grey hair
And jeered at what they saw her bear
    Within her womb:
'Are you that old man's wife?' they said.
   'Who made you fatten so?'
But Mary simply bowed her head
   And went out in the snow.
        Then gladly, yet sadly,
        They left the inn behind,
        While jeering and sneering
        The others drank and dined.

Then Mary whispered in his ear,
She felt her time of birth was near
    And shook with cold.
Splinters of ice hung from the trees
Creaking like guilty memories
    Of crimes untold.
They passed a cave beside the road
  Where bullocks froze in sleep,
While crisp outside the starlight glowed
  Upon a midden heap.
      But tearful and fearful
      She throbbed within her gown:
      So gently, intently,
      He lifted Mary down.

Leading their donkey to the cave
They took the shelter that it gave
    For Mary's bed;
And gathering her road-stained dress
She lay within a rock recess
    Where straw was spread.
Then stable animals drew round
  To keep her body warm,
While hard across the frozen ground
  Jolted old Joseph's form.
      Both riding and sliding
      Along the hardened track
      He worried, and hurried
      To bring a midwife back.

The busy town was wide awake,
And Joseph had to shout to make
     His message clear;
For Caesar had proclaimed from Rome
Each should return to his own home
     From far and near
To be enrolled; and streets thick-packed
   With bodies barred his way
Till an old nurse, her voice age-cracked,
   Heard what he had to say.
          Then hearing, and fearing
          Lest Mary came to harm,
          She scolded, and folded
          Some blankets on her arm.

But when they came back to the hill
A blinding cloud came down to fill
     The cave with light
And dazzled them, until at last
The flame, its blaze of fury passed,
     Shone clear and bright.
They trembled like two hawthorn clumps
   That waver on a dyke
Where willows pollarded to stumps
   Bend for a lightning strike.
          But shaking and waking
          They found her undistressed;
          For sweetly, discreetly,
          Her baby sucked her breast.

Some streaks of day spread through the sky
As Mary sang a lullaby
    To her new-born.
Linnets and starlings perched around
Waking all nature with their sound
    And din of dawn:
The orchards and the olive-groves
  Filled with fresh-waking noise,
And early cattle passed in droves
  Driven by sleepy boys.
      Then tramping and stamping
      Some shepherds asked if they
      Might enter; they sent her
      A lamb this holy-day.

One star remained, although the sun
Softened the snow-webs night had spun,
    When from the East
Out of the dawn, like ripened grain
Rippling a field, a camel train
    Thundered, released
From wandering and pilgrimage;
  For now three men appeared:
One young, one silvery with age,
  One dark, with uncut beard.
      Descending and bending
      To enter with their store
      Of treasure, with pleasure
      They spread it on the floor.

Symbols of royal gods of old,
Time-honoured mysteries untold,
    And myrrh of death
Surrounded Jesus where he played,
While gulls and meadow pipits strayed
    Catching their breath
In chokes of song; and Mary gazed
    Too full with happiness
To speak, while Joseph stood amazed
    Staring and motionless.
        Now sweeping and keeping
        The cave from mud and mire,
        With cinder and tinder
        The shepherds made a fire.

When evening came a hidden breeze
Wafted within a swarm of bees
    That filled the air
With sounds that seemed to sink and swell,
Like music in an ocean shell
    Or badger's lair.
A shadow hovered, still, outside
    As though afraid to come,
Until at length it ceased to hide:
    And the bees ceased to hum.
        Then, wary, a hairy
        Rough form came from the street,
        And listful, yet wistful,
        Laid reed-pipes at his feet.

And late that night, when all had left,
A helmsman nodding on his chest
    Woke with alarm:
A sudden wind from off the shore
Beat on his sails a bitter roar
    That broke the calm.
He saw his rigging torn away
  And left without a shred,
And heard a loud lamenting say,
  'Tell out great Pan is dead!'
     Then swirling and hurling
     Its thunder of that name,
     With calling and falling
     The wind sank as it came.

Cambridge, February 1962

PLAINSONG

In memory of
Angus and David

'Reapt ere half ripe, finisht ere half begunne.'

A viper's cored within this apple-world,
And sunning through the orchards of the mind
Choosing only the red and ripest fruit—
The bruised ignored, the bitter thrown aside—
No more tells true; it satisfies no more.
A second's dead. Two warm and living friends
Wasting in mud and loam: suddenly snuffed
On reaching manhood. One, and now another.
Why, why oh why is this bitterness of doubt,
This thud of guilt and loneliness of despair,
Impossible, titanic weight of a universe
Balanced to try each one of us in turn?

I must not pose, colour or decorate
And clothe an ugly fact: lament Adonis,
Or mourn on Lycidas's golden urn.
As memory grows distortion will encroach,
And the brute impact of shattering moment on soul
Borne in the heart alone, but labelled sorrow,
Will fade: yet while it cuts into my brain
I'll make a map of torment; bend the verse
And wrest from it an iron ore of truth
Stripped of accretions made from imitations:
Lift up that flap of the brain and journey in
To grip the bit and bridle of the heart.

I've said I'll strike no attitude—and yet
Saying that may itself be one more pose
No truer than those first ones stripped away:
Or do I like, enjoy the sound of grief
And say I say I mourn? Away, mind-spider!
This creeping ivy's curst. I doubt my doubts,
And meanings have no meaning when intellect
Battens on raw emotion: one more way
Creation tries to hide, to shift the burden,
Seeking a screen in arguments on terms,
Fleeing the core and crawling round the skin
Wide of the bitter heritage within.

Sorrow humiliates, is hard to bear
Because the mightiest structures of the mind
Prove groundless; vanish in a puff of smoke;
And puny man retaliates in grief
Throwing his weightiest words in the empty air;
A whistling ant on an orange. Banished from home,
His comforting illusions swept away,
His petty pride and patronage destroyed,
He faces the unknown—yet still re-forms
Newer delusions for those cut apart
When shock shewed all had lied. The spear of fear
Burns to the bone until he builds once more.

Anatomies of grief, wild posturings,
Word-spun distractions, analytic sleights,
Convention and invention breeding still
Unfelt belief, untested promises—
All wrestling factions in the dark extreme
Passed by—attention drawn away with skill
To surface crusts spanning the torn abyss:
These are mere tricks; mirrors in place of glass,
Telling no more than happiness requires;
Puppets of showmen fanning childhood thoughts
With idle tales by hayricks in the sun;
Bolting the door that opens on the void.

To realize each moment as it comes,
Naked, for what it is, will be my task.
This chair set back within a book-lined room,
That creaking movement of the tree outside
Stripped to its branches while the wind blows cold;
A dust-filled crack between two flooring-boards:
The crow on the roof. Tomorrow will be spring,
Yet grey-white clouds are piling in the sky
Like down: the snow is staying late this year,
And dusk soon falls. No proof has come of spring,
No swarming crowds of peewits in the fields:
Only this hollow deadness in my chest.

And yet, some night ago I sat just here
Gazing out through this window. Then the dawn
Had scarcely touched the sky. Faint, earliest light
Tipped the trees white and froze each hedge and bush
With needle-blue of frosted handiwork.
The scarecrow on his crutch was crisp with cold,
And water butts stood shackled in thick ice.
Slowly full day had spread across the sky
Freeing the water from the chilled spring-well,
Filling each wood with life and waking cocks
Till far away a homing owl had called
His cry that silent slaughtering was done.

Then all was fresh. Imagination clothed
Each fact of nature in its simplest joy.
No irons had been heated for the soul;
No snare or mesh had sprung and trapped the pulse
Each single creature woke inside my heart.
Now evening blows and sleet begins to fall
And I must force corroding images
Away, lest grief becomes a luxury.
Daylight has nearly gone, yet clear outside
A cart-truck runs: a course that I must take.
The window's dark. A dead leaf taps the glass.
I'll drag myself alone into the night.

Cold lashes strike my face. The track is hard
And slippery; storm wind cuts through my hair
In rifts, while far away dim city lights
Beckon me on like fishing-lamps at sea.
Storms in my mind should cease while icy gusts
Hold well at bay all but immediate thoughts—
Dark hollows full of weeds, my sodden hair,
This bitter rain and massacre of wind:
Music of elements that scours the soul
And makes the muscles pull their proper strength.
This blast will clear my brain and fight the growth
Of weird embellishments that breed despair.

Dark of the soul, darkness soul-bright:
The image echoing-chamber of the mind
Twisted in cramp that tightens its clamp—
Tear-blind in sight of its goal.

Numb to the battering wind
Oblivious of pain
Only the dead beat in the head
And images that fight
Contorted, grotesque, like shadows that camp-fire the night.

On to the distant lights
Though canvas stretches till split;
Heaven torn as a world is stillborn
And hatred of gods gutters our phantom out.
The dragon of night burns the bridges and torments the trees
Which shoulder a burden that cracks on the traveller's knees.

Shelter of buildings; city streets at last:
Landscape of suffering worse than my own,
Man-made mortality. This chapel door
With gildings marked in subtle filigree
Will shield from buffeting. From the far end
Boyish vitality soars to the roof
Worrying out each sleeping spider's web.
The climbing words sink down into my ears
Like silkworms, calling, 'He that shall endure
To the end . . .'. A leech has slipped down on my sleeve
And thirds descending end the anthem's tale.
Once more I'll fight the bawling wind and hail.

This is the city boundary, where the lamps
And houses cluster in one final knot
That's flattered with a flower-bedded tree.
On, blustering strides! Have pity on the lambs
Born on the fen. Muster your forces for
An onslaught on the coffin-leaded laws
That rule this meaningless and cancered globe
In socket-eyed, gigantic merriment
Like grinning cormorants with new-hatched eggs,
Or madmen leaning on a laddered man
Who gazes frantic at the swimming ground
While stifling heart-pants cataract his eyes.

The railway-crossing. Now the fen itself
Stretches out like a glacier of ooze
Waded by buried gods, who shake their hill
With sleepless tossing and dream-stifled fears
And trudge the peat beyond the dyke in storms,
Drinking in serried darkness like a draught
That drunken demons throw across the sun
Blanketing clouds to rifle virgin souls
Who sink in fear before their tyrant strength.
The piping gleemen of the tempest-dance
Shrouding the earth and waking walrus-wastes
Hunt down the deer that streaks across the sky.

I know a lonely inn where two streams meet
To make a river, where a goat is tied;
A ferry moors; and broken window-frames
Offer their thin resistance to the storm:
Unsheltered coltsfoot shiver on the bank,
And bindweed claws and chokes the fishy reeds.
Now that the wind has held its breath, I'll make
My way there; try to find pure solitude,
That silent space of quiet that enfolds
The vacuum kingdom of the realm within;
Far from all cry of crippling appetites
That race exhausted blood about the veins;

And cool this cook and windmill of a mind
A moment, thinking of past summer days
Spent by that inn, when silver willows grew
Across a brook dense with strange river-weeds;
Watching a stickleback weave in and round,
Hover, and flick his fin, while sun-hard clay
Gleamed brick-white when soft winds blew corn in lanes;
The sleeping snail that sunbathed on a log;
The vole that held a twig between his teeth
Keeping it dry aloft, as on he swam
Steered by his heirloom tail; the crickets' cry;
The fledgeling that rebelled and lost his life:

The widening sky that served the setting sun
Platformed like polished tables from a feast
Of dazed and drunken ancient deities,
When healths pledged high, and crimson wine spilled
    down
Tracing bold, airy fables of past days,
Blazing a tapestry for creeping man.
So often I have knelt to watch a plant
Or insect, or a tiny animal,
Zoo-beast or meadow-grazer, fish or fly,
And known I felt with every living growth
That feels: a shiny toad or woolly sheep.
Cruelty razor-cut my arteries.

The lonely fens are dark tonight
  And swept by wind and rain.
The watcher in the lonely house
  Deaf to the window-pane.

A wanderer with a hurricane lamp
  Moves by the riverside.
A mother mourns in the candlelight
  Silent and glassy-eyed.

She's laid his naked body out
  And lit the candles round.
The blackened river swells outside:
  Her mourning makes no sound.

'Halloo! Come, open up the door!
  The rain has pierced my skin!'
With fingers numb of feeling
  She lets the traveller in.

'These many hours I've watched with you
  Yet still the wicks burn bright!'
'I gave you shelter from the storm:
  Watch till the morning light.'

The lonely fens are desolate
  The house but bricks and straw,
And empty winds throughout that house
  Will blow for evermore.

This ferry-boat must do—where are the oars?
Away from this derelict ghost-haunted inn
And mourning candle-glow. The dawn is queer:
No breeze. The goat's stopped munching. Now's the time
When geese stretch up to hiss, and distant bells
Sound clearer; cocks crow; soot falls in the fire,
And cats wash back their ears. Rain's on the way
And I alone within this little boat,
Oarless, and bitterly tired. You bulrushes,
Bearded and wrapped with fears that weigh you down,
Give me your blessing. Stones and swiftest birds,
If I must suffer still, defiled within,

Broken and beaten, give me power to bear
All that must come! My coward body shakes
And water smears my eyes in molten glass.
This speeding, wheaten, clay-gold river speeds,
Carries me on. The drumbeat in my eyes
Frightens me. Every world-born life that dies
Is not forced to endure this cruel sport
Of elemental kings whose thumbs turn down!
What is the index to your catalogue
Of punishment? Are fuel faggots still
To come in sacramental sacrifice,
My victim reflex analysed in fire?

The thoughts of love in a whirlwind
Cry out from the antique shore
To strike the nerve of the heart of man for evermore.

The cries of the frozen sparrow
Pinched in spears of snow
Waste in the winding winds where the arctic mirrors blow.

Half through our life, half through our dark,
Gusts on the flickering fen—
The madness of wind and storm scatters the breath of men.

What is that speck in the north? That growing cloud
Approaching, blackening the air? The midnight bull
Mighty, primeval, bursting from the sky
To butt this worthless bubble globe aside
Trampling the fair and circus of mankind
Like clover in a field: thirsting for death
His horns rip up the heavens and cyclones swoop
Wresting up trees and rocks, swamping the land
Beneath a sheet of sea. Towers tottering
Bend and crash. A ship splits down its back,
Though still this nutshell boat flees in the vast
Ungovernable splendour of the storm.

The contemplation of a universe
In chaos is the holocaust of joy
And hatred, fear, pride, laughter, pain,
Clear vision of destruction vouched to this
Trans-sanity. All things boast equal terms
Beneath the unchaining elements that strain,
Rage, and batter this defenceless earth.
Titanic battle of giant squid and whale
In lonely ice-wastes down the winter nights,
Monsters that scatter snowcaps, shrink in size
To a thimble where two pliant gnats make love
Measured beside this crown of final death.

The sun on the broken mountain blesses the final sea
That washes away the muddy foam of man-made futility,
The devastating and recreating waters that cover the earth
Promise a new healing refreshment for elemental dearth.
        A mighty view of sun, season, earth, sea, and sky
Bound in one chain of perfect love, joyous that man must
    die,
Sends out a silent, ageless oath: that the new will be
    undefiled,
And all the archaic world unknown in the joy of their
    new-born child.

Alpha Cottage, Trumpington, March 1962

Experimental Sonnets

Note

*Most of the sonnets in this sequence change the
traditional form by bringing many of the rhyme-
words in from the end of lines, usually to the
centre. (Formal centre-rhyme is first used
in this book for the poem preceding these
sonnets,* Plainsong.)

I

In order that some splinter may remain
Of all that glory, here, in my poor verse,
Let me evoke the strained, satanic pain
Of vivisecting parting, and rehearse
Those moments of brief immortality
Lying oblivious and locked in one,
The songs and river gliding past us free
And unrestrained; the warm cathedral sun;
Our wooded walks, our tiptoed nights of joy
After the academic pleasantries;
Dark candle-light and soaring solo boy;
The soft perfection of your dancing eyes.
    But this, sweet lady, is a country new,
    And all the world I'll recreate, for you.

II

No, I've not slept or rested, though it must
Be dawn by now, for daylight hints the room;
The clocks have kept each patient quarter-hour
And etched my brow with music of contempt:
Ten thousand times that starlight's pushed my lids
To demonstrate a breeze is not your hair
Trailing in lines across my cheek to tease
And half-create your darkling mockery.
What anodyne perturbs this semi-globe
That I, one little fragment of the night,
In moonshine of a lover's fantasy
Can only whittle down the ember hours
　　　Lying awake? Imaginings grow worse,
　　　While God plays snooker with the universe.

III

Dragging my wandering and battered feet
Along the towpath by the Cambridge stream,
Reading or writing verse, violent, sweet,
Living on memory that seems a dream,
I draw what sustenance still gives me life
Not from the worldly dust for which men sweat,
Grinding in busy streets—the smiling strife
And vampire business-deals that breed on debt;
Not from the eunuch-mystic's incense-smoke,
Nor from high hopes of honourable age,
Justice, or social platitude—that cloak
Invoked by petty minds to ape the sage:
　　　Lacking such spurs, another makes me burn;
　　　Look in the left-hand column, dear, and learn.

IV

Sick with this black despair of loving you,
Absent, desperate for your company,
Your voice, your eyes; knowing you with another,
Snared by a mocking pack that's hunting still,
Your undefended bait their leering sport,
Their grinned and greasy sty new-fanged your trap,
Time becomes fever-bout, fleshed broken glass,
A purgatory pace around the skull,
A plain with walls and ceiling closing in
As hope ebbs out and candles gutter down
And such disgrace scars incapacity
It scalds raw, dislocated, ransacked mind
    Until I know there is no deeper hell
    Than this, sweet Christ! of loving you too well.

V

What can I do, what can I think or say
Without you? What tight wrench of mind can twist
Even one simple operation plain
Undedicated to your distant thought,
Unshadowed by your lightning; unrehearsed
In preparation for that fleeting time
When we shall meet, only to part, and break
New anvil tortures on my nut-cracked knees,
Freeing the pit to leer its blackness up,
Greet and invite, shackle us to its bars,
Till the next kingfisher moment cut the dark
In meteor career down to the sea?
    Strange comment by that phantom circumstance
    On splendour of man's insignificance.

VI

There are some moments when the mind is scorched
More than a kettle down a baby's face,
Or spark in eye. Then hesitating trust,
Trying to settle into confidence
In spite of injuries sustained before
That transcendental meeting, is exposed,
Undefended, unrestrained, in love
And vulnerable, keeping nothing hid.
A whip-crack at that delicately balanced
Perfected instant cataracts the nerve
And snaps the backbone like a cygnet's wing
In tortured wince and catastrophic end.
      If this prime, envied bud of life is ours,
      Why do we catalogue our thorns and briars?

VII

Something—a restless fear beneath my brain
Hints that all is not well; the parting miles
Like prison warders jeer at confidence,
Strike on a jarring bell their furlongs up
And cynicize that distance should keep trust:
'Love like a natural scene evaporates
When the horizon's clanged its gates!' They set
Panicking thoughts to scream along the nerves
Like blackboard chalk, or sparrow stamped upon
By hob-nailed schoolboy fighting with a friend,
Ceasing, appalled; their walk in horror hushed.
Dread, and irrational fright disturb the dark.
      I say our faith is mutual, and sure;
      And yet I fear, lest yours may not endure.

VIII

From the creation of that evening, when
Shipwrecked by chaosed winds, our new-touched lives
Flashed and leaped high in one transcendent flame,
Not isolation, distance, weakness, fear,
Restless, cycloning minds, physically
Separated by irony of past
Yet anchored each within the other's brain—
Mockery, silence, disease, temptation; nothing
Has sullied absolute relationship.
Yet this leech world conspires against such light,
Seeks to snuff down and squeeze under its slime
Those who are not brutalized to despair.
    Will may corrode and pain can split the bone;
    Nothing eradicates what we have known.

IX

Is it a certain gentleness, a touch
Of unmistakable nobility
Under your curtain and façade of life
That breaks discourtesy, compels respect?
Or exercise of unobtrusive taste;
A tact, finding beneath this hell of strain,
Instinctively, one small. elusive joy
Guttering in the heath-storm of the mind;
And cherishes, until the rain-blown spark
Curls to new radiance, throws back the night,
Beacons from hill to hill, transcends the sun,
Hurls suffering to insignificance?
    Is it a certain quality of soul?
    Yes, all of these; for you have made me whole.

X

Was that white shape that lurched out of the night
To suffocate our windscreen, breathing on
Into the perched and blinded loneliness,
An owl? No prate of peopled England here.
The headlights catch the cautious rabbits' play
And romp them roadsiding, to widow past,
Unkiss the shroud and lift the latch of dark;
Probing the bosomed, cat's-eyed mist ahead,
Half-formed and damp; thick, intermittent, gone.
This far-past-midnight world of deerhorned trunks
And unrepentant fields so utterly ours
We tread the edge of promise with the dawn.
New senses register. Re-live all these
As moving emblems of our sympathies.

XI

When day's ranked, echoing pageantry is furled,
Yielding me benediction of your breast,
A prisoner flanked in nipple sentinels,
Full dereliction by the universe
Cannot disturb this bedside candle's flame,
Or break the quiet of your mystery:
No war perturb, no butcher-doubts usurp
The spirit's diet of love's harvestry.
Your pillowed calm breeds life, and can renew
Oceans and continents in a caress
Where all the motions of eternity
Touch the still trembling pity of your peace.
Beside such miracle, why, earth's crammed store
To rim of outer space is beggared poor.

XII

Grappling with fear, riding the razor-edge
Of being, hesitant whether to exist,
Doubtful of wintry world, warm without form,
Outside the cradle and bier of mammocked creation;
Lonely impulse, featherbreath tangent of God
Forcing your unuttered hint like a wedge through a planet
Into our lives, illumine experience;
Nexus of void and becoming, make your great choice:
Warrant our waiting, anchored in tangible substance,
A fardel of drives and inherited flesh, alone
Reaching beyond the cloyed and derangeable cosmos,
Nervepoint of mating, a galaxy thumbscrewed in poise.
    Essence essential, arrogate hope's dismay;
    Receive the catastrophe of human day.

XIII

A towel; suitcase; this a hotel room.
Each object, élite, curiously numb:
Clean, empty place of unreality,
All singly neat. Mad traffic hurtling on,
Metal, below. The bed's bare winding-sheets.
Alone for time to come: then why sit down
To throw an understatement on a page—
How can I further explore heartbreak's pit
And come back sane? No: let the new scab form;
Stay numb. Cross-lock the door. Force the hand still;
Unless articulation stir, to fill
The icy moment at the heart of pain.
    Is there a reason behind human care?
    What is the acreage of its despair.

93

XIV

Aware, across this mountain baritoned
Moss-bearded waterfall, that as you bend
Carefree beside the green-eyed, weeping race,
Even the elusive moments comprehend
Only in retrospect; becoming, change:
That thought destroys, though desperately preserves;
And each flecked leaf's baptized in a free grace
Caught in your unaware, cascading joy.
Suddenly sensitive that we're alone—
Each movement stilled new in your arm or eye
Aeons and civilizations cannot own
Again; that you are holy, and unique.
    Watching such value stand up in the rain,
    Aware in truth, I know myself profane.

XV

Yes, you are flesh and blood all right. My God!
And do I know it. Scorn convention's track
Yet follow it, inclining to conform
When cautious pressure from a hackneyed world
Threats in my absence. So, proud stamina
Steps into line and licks the boots of law;
Simpers authority and worships straw;
Ventures, in prudence; pioneers, in bed—
Jesus! What zombie's this? What carcass-thief
Postures this attitude? Nods, mutters back
Exactitude of platitude, and fears
A pontiff's ransom of unborn regret?
    Is the high lark, dawn's song-drenched accolade,
    Only a small grey hopper round a spade?

XVI

With you I can do anything. Without,
The sodden shroud, the rough planks, hard beneath,
Over stared eyes, binding the elbows in;
Fouled, waterlogging dew; the white, gorged worm;
Inevitable dark; rank, crumpled flesh;
Grit, blinding dust and everlasting cold
Feel. But death's mockery hours—these we have shared
In downy warmth, where want, and wounds, and cares,
And world's oppressions break no breathing calm,
Disturb no dockleaf, still no finger's trace.
When courtesy and constancy are matched,
And love of beauty makes you beautiful,
    Then mailed fist of fate can smash our skulls,
    For we can ridicule all death annuls.

XVII

Our passion is no bold extravagance
Or cultivation of hyperbole;
Nor fashioned in that rhetoric that finds
Fresh startling merit in obscurity.
There is no poetry save what we live,
And tone of voice, and form, are personal;
An individual imperative
Bred of no choice, but brought out like the grain
Elicited with seasoned polishing
Of teak. So if, in these hewn trunks of mine
You recognize our accents, know you bring
Fulfilment in the marrow of the spine:
    And let our love, like deepest art, be seen
    To be inevitable, strong, and clean.

XVIII

As our fates navigate their destined route
In modulations of intensity,
And times necessitate a change of time
Not in relationship but counterpoint;
As each new stroke is added by the brush
Of that practitioner of artistry,
And though we wear the cloak, yet do not know
The composition, or the epigraph;
As each new moment beats upon the pulse,
Let us resolve to try whatever comes,
Not in heat's self-paralysis of hate,
But with compassion's quiet certainty;
    And neither flinch, nor find across our course
    Memories of unmitigated remorse.

XIX

Night wins. The realizing dark
Granites that knife along eternity.
Who sins? What is this idle guilt?
Father forgive, by Thy Gethsemane.
Eat, drink, riot today and forget!
By Thine agony and bloody sweat—
Come, try at the wheel; spin, wager a bet!
Ransom my core from catastrophic debt.
If I must live with this full-earned abyss,
If I must face my moral holocaust,
Father, forgive, though I know what I do,
Forgive my sin against the Holy Ghost.
    The worst is done; the last brutality:
    And mine the sole responsibility.

XX

As in her grief a mother cannot clean
The fingermarks left on the window-pane,
But finds relief in sitting for a while
Where he with deft impatience on the floor
Tugged off his shoes, still knotted by the fire;
Half-waits the tottering walk; picks up the coat
Dropped when fresh news was spilling to be shared
In nonsense-babbling talk of outstretched toy:
As at such times a father cloisters up
His thoughts, attempts to play the comforter,
Awkwardly; climbs beneath the roof to search
For papers that he knows may not be there:
    As such emotion dreads to be betrayed,
    So, in the silent grief, one part's afraid.

XXI

Outside, stuttering hate snarls down the blade
As a pneumatic drill rapes the dead quay:
Inside, recreated, as a shaft
Of black light penetrates the opened soul.
Somewhere a plumber saws his piece of lead;
A ribbed and creaking boat heels on the sand;
Nearer, a drawing-pin studs in the eye
Of mind, as vessel, float, all disappear.
Down, down as they go, the bubbles rise,
The drowned's report upon experience.
Up, up expanding hope replies
Until exploded by the drill's retort.
    Ah, comedy divine, man's tragedy—
    Why make us gambol in our agony?

XXII

Should we preserve intensity alone?
The string vibrating at the 'cello's bridge?
Or stretch to nerve the fingerboard's full range
In orchestrating waste's cacophonics?
Is poignancy of beauty's transience
As time runs over an apple in the stream—
The hesitancy of a summer's dusk
When night-stock stuns with scent—ours to forgo?
Must we desert court-ladies on the grass,
Their sunlit-dappled breasts and lovers' lutes?
The skill of craftsman-wrought, firm, rounded themes;
The guests of Mozart, Purcell, and Watteau?
    Bear with me if I leave such scenes behind:
    The dark offstage preoccupies my mind.

XXIII

If mechanism's throb betrays the mind
But once, then restless empiry's collapsed;
The vermin rob immortal artistry
And wisdom, fleshless, reels into the dust.
Grey waste of intricacy's heritage,
Endowed to growth and destined to decay,
Disburses melody, like pollen blown,
Loath to depart yet powerless to stay.
Abrasive anger at such impotence
To help the frailer by diviner part
Engineers atrophy of maimed desire
And nails inevitable reconciled.
    So dialectics isolate the flaw.
    So small a key unlocks so great a door.

XXIV

The breaking dawn, the cry upon the bed;
Tottering infancy and gangling youth;
Mandarin manhood. Anarchy of age
At last, raving, forlorn and groping back,
Fearing the icy wind's strangling grip,
To corridors of constant journeying;
The secret prides and flattering self-denials;
Laconic labials, fantasy's deceit;
Books, Bibles, bidets; halls, hills, cottages;
Flow and ebb of bodily seasons' tides;
Those motley macaronics day and night;
Companions—all the panoply of rust.
    No intermission from this pantomime
    Till termination bring an end to time.

XXV

And can it be? Has all that splendour passed—
Was it too pure for weak mortality?
Was I demanding, hoping it might last;
Now disillusioned with humanity?
It seems impossible so firm a joy,
A love so rooted in a summer's day,
Shared tasks, shared wanderings, should like a toy
A child has wearied of be tossed away.
And can this paper be the last that you
Will hold of mine, these words end passion's qualms?
Darkness must touch these eyes now, as we knew,
And lonely nights lend you their empty arms.
    Strange how the mutability of things
    Evaporates all man's imaginings.

Madrigals

HEARTBREAK OF JOY

Heartbreak of joy, my only peace,
Living thread in a wilderness of maze,
As the cider press crushes the screaming juice
Take these broken words into your gaze.

You are all strength, stronger than light itself,
The natural power that pulses sap through veins,
The driving life-force of this dying world
That holds the sun and stars in tender chains.

My life, in truth, I lay it at your feet,
Though horror still maggots within this skull.
Doctor of lacerated brains, I weep
I have no more than all I have to spill,

To recompense, and thank and breed for you,
Tenderest miracle and torments' balm;
Would I could amputate my limbs to show
Determined sacrifice blasts shadows' harm;

And yet they do not reach the inner heart—
They cannot quarry where the mountains heave;
Blind, yes and gouge—they strike with sadist's art;
They cannot break our blessing and our love.

INNOCENCE

Bells, bells calling
Snow, snow falling
Soft wintry wind—
Yes, I have sinned.

VENUS AND THE POET

He   Is there future in the past,
Hazard once the die is cast?
Or in parting can there be
Dying immortality
From chance words that yet remain,
Evanescence in a stain?

Must a circumstantial blow
Murder what was born to grow
While the passing wintry days
Echo 'All decays, betrays . . .'?
Love and poetry sustain
Small defence against the rain.

She   Come, leave mutability,
Lie me down beneath this tree;
Surging spring laughs doubts to flight,
Strength increases with delight
Till, where Absence long has lain,
My lover reaps his ripened grain.

IMPROMPTU

Gentle lady, in your face
Dances every human grace
And the sunshine of your eyes
Breaks the dawn in Paradise—
If you will not share this song
A living moment's lost, and gone.

A DEFINITION

Love is imaginative sympathy
Pure in unlimited intensity
And constant love the truest chastity—
    So, even such,
    Your touch.

STILL LIFE

Afternoon sun; she lies upon the bed
Breast down: ripe apple plucked by ecstasy.

SONNET

Your love, perfection's crown, to me is strength,
Harbour and sanctuary after storm;
My only-wished renown; the breadth and length
Of all ideals, and their shaping form.
I know this is not new, a thousand men
Have made their loves immortal in a song,
Paid court and flattered, wooed in verse, and then
Sewn up unbounded passion with a thong;
And yet, and yet . . . Why is it each believes
His is the incontestable delight?
We cannot measure how another grieves—
How then reflect our universe of light?
    Yet, knowing this, I say in spite of all
    That no man's heart was ever half so full.

THE WALLED GARDEN

Careful! Now salt is spilt across the board.
But what's the tracery these grains inscribe?
Look where the sky's resplendent overlord
Strokes the walled-garden sunbather his bride.
See how she lies: her hands beneath her head
One knee half-raised to part the warming beams
Sultry and young, a breeder gently bred,
The distillation of ripe nature's means.
Come, stare no more. No prying eyes may graze
On innocence that has not learned to cloy.
Cursed be the man whose moral-surfeit brays
Sully the living moments of her joy!
    These grains of salt: and memory is stung—
    And this the most disturbing picture sung.

WHEN YOU ARE MINE

When you are mine
The quicks beneath the fingernails
Blanch.

When you undress
The skin sings like a comb, and stings the glow
To every feeling corner of the brain.

When you look down,
Your hair flung loose, and thumbs slipped under straps
You ease the full, rich load
And watch your tender lover's buds burst free
For suckling and delight;

And as you bend
Twisting to guide the stud-gripped fastener loose—
Roll down the knee-raised stocking, and ease free
Holding, surrounding silk, to leave
To freedom's air your down:

So, as you stand
Pooled in discarded clothes, your eyes look up
Unafraid, to accept
Your woman's heritage of fulfilled strength

Know that what splits the nerve of certainty
Is your spontaneous nakedness of mind.

SONG

Lift your hair from the water
    And lie and let it lap
Till bubbles rise round nipples
    To wanton with the tap.
What modesty's offended
    When beauty's hid from view?
What artistry more splendid
    Than you?

If cleanliness of body
    Shows purity of mind,
Come, let this soap excite you
    Before, between, behind;
Let dalliance have leisure
    And luxury caress
Till elemental pleasure
    Possess.

Come to me naked darling,
    Spread pillows on the bed:
I break this rarest perfume
    To bless new maidenhead.
Come warm, refreshed and trembling
    With joy that dares delight
To fathom through dissembling
    Tonight.

THE BALLAD OF BRENDAN BEHAN

Come gather round me, sweethearts,
　　And lovers, lift your heads;
Come, old men from the fireside,
　　And children from your beds;
Come, neighbours, friends, and travellers,
　　And hear me sing a stave
Of a laughing boy from Dublin
　　Now lying in his grave.

For Brendan loved his city,
　　The place where he was born,
He'd toast her health in Mooney's
　　From twilight round till morn;
From morn again to twilight
　　He'd laugh and sing and say
'Mock all the world, my darlin's,
　　But back the I.R.A.'

They put him into prison
　　When he was sweet fifteen,
And innocent of whiskey,
　　And only knew potheen:
In Liverpool they locked him
　　For smuggling contraband,
For forging of a passport,
　　And fighting for his land.

Eight long years being over,
　　The Borstal boy was free;
He kissed the screws and sold his shoes
　　To sail the homeward sea.
He quenched his English prison thirst
　　With English prison pay,
And wrote a laughing prison book,
　　And then a hanging play.

Joan Littlewood in London,
    She sent a telegram:
'Come join us in our theatre,
    Come back, me darlin' man!'
Soon Brendan's name is blazoned
    In flashing neon lights.
The laughing boy buys drinks for all
    Throughout the winter nights.

He scribbled as he gargled
    Another singing play,
About a cockney soldier
    Shot by the I.R.A.
His fame crossed the Atlantic,
    His laughter shook New York:
But still he loved his Dublin,
    His Galway, and his Cork.

A Gaelic baby daughter
    Grinned up a new-born smile:
'Be Jasus! I'll forsake the malt
    And take up milk awhile.'
He snatched his pen, and wrote again
    Two books about his friends,
Then quaffed a can at The Shaky Man
    To join and make amends.

Oh all you wives and lovers,
    Take heed unto my tale;
Follow the fate of the laughing boy
    Locked in an English gaol;
The boy with laughter in his eyes,
    And liquor in his veins:
And love like him, forgive like him,
    Till Death knocks out your brains.

Courtesy of Anglia T.V.
Transmission 20th March 1964

BALLAD FROM 'RIOT', AN ABANDONED PLAY

(Time, 1816)

When Jack was a youngster he had a fine house,
And linen and carpets and beds;
He fished and he hunted and shot his own grouse,
Drank vintage and baked his own breads.
But Johnny-boy-soldier went off to the wars
All dressed in his tunic and boots;
And when he came back they had ransacked his stores
And pulled up his trees by the roots.

Lie down, my small darling, I'll sing you a tune,
                     for shadows move dark in the wood;
Your daddy is out by the light of the moon,
                     and he walks where the gamekeeper stood.

Now Johnny-boy-soldier, he rides all alone
And knows every track of the fen;
He's a bright baby daughter and lady called Joan,
And a coat cut in velvet again.
Oh, the inn-keepers welcome his tap at the door,
And the millers mount guard on their mill:
But they'll never catch Johnny in ten years or more
Though the gibbet stands high on the hill.

Lie down, my small darling, no candle must flame,
                     lie close as you hear what I'll sing;
For Johnny your daddy has got a new name
                     which the wayfarers call Captain Swing.

SONNET INSCRIBED IN A COPY OF ANDREW YOUNG'S *THE POET AND THE LANDSCAPE*

Come, take this book with me when winter winds
Blow boisterous through the crucifixion trees
And tread again those pathways in our minds,
Our summer's foliage of memories.
Why, we have set the sun on Helpston church,
Sought out the resting-place of weary Crabbe,
Searched in the roof of Diss, where hawks would perch,
Seen where King Charles and Rochester would drab.
Ah, many ways we've wandered, you and I,
Treading the varied haunts of poetry—
From where Ben Bulben merges mist with sky
To Blunden's Suffolk, mill-board reverie.
　　　Each place we visit's ours, because your mind
　　　Makes the past live till life itself seems kind.

ENDPIECE

　　　The restless rivers wind and flow
　　　And wintry winds of fortune blow
　　　　　Piercing this body's tree;
　　　Yet, while it stands, its roots still strong,
　　　Take in your hands these leaves of song,
　　　So, when the shades grow cold and long,
　　　　　You may remember me.

THE TRUTH

By the toccata of this autumn's wane,
By all this headstrong girasole of leaf,
By the bare winter truth none will remain
When the fanged frost has split the frozen sheaf,
By this fen's ploughed vernacular of weeds,
I bring you permanence, as all recedes.

We know that in few fleeting years mankind will be no
   more,
The barrel of humanity run dry, the grain crushed on a
   granite floor,
We know that in man's evolution lies his fatal flaw.

Yet, in this empire of necessity,
Of ravaged autumn preluding the spring,
Of mock heroic man's effrontery
Cradling extinction, permanence can sing:
Season outlives the species, yet is evanescent too;
Only perception of this fact and human love are true.

FOR GEORGINA

aged three

Laughing little buttercup
  Sunbeam of the meadows
Ear of wheat among the corn
  Fledgeling of the hedgerows

Mimic of the open air
  Seeking the way the wind went
Stern to escape, swift to return
  Fearlessly dependent

May you ever hide and skip
  By Cherwell or by Granta
Innocent as you are now
  My goldenhaired enchanter.

5th September 1965

THE PASSIONATE GOATHERD

Come love with me and be my life
And be my mistress and my wife
And in your lover you will find
Outrageous joy in humankind.

Your bridal gown will be the dawn
When first light tips the golden corn,
Before those rougher beams of day
Have pushed the insects from their hay.

Your veil, to whisper down your cheeks,
Be spider-spun five-hundred weeks;
The shoes that clasp your milk-white toes
Those shells where mermaids find repose,

And breezes round you as you walk
Will pull each lip to hear it talk;
Fresh grass about you as you dance
Peep sideways up with sparkling glance.

Your bridegroom's ring, be Constant Love;
The daisy-chain Content, your glove;
And running streams on every side
Will ripple sunshine down my bride.

If in this dowry there is art
To race your blood and beat your heart,
Come live with me in sweet delight:
And love me, sweet, this very night.

HOSPITAL DAWN

So the pulse beats and slows,
The daylight seeps, creeping
Crosswise against the bandage of the mind,
Miraculously lightening
Load upon nodal nerve of lid-red eyes
Fluttering, like kerbside to a skull
New-dashed in crash, not yet abed and cold.

So the revulsion glows
Sky-blind, and it must feel its way along
The daily parapet, nor yet
Look down, nor up, nor yet perceive at all,
So small
That mental island we call sanity.

SPELL FOR SAFE RETURN

Stay, waves, stay, cease your inconstant crying,
Trace no increasing tears upon the sand,
Fall, winds, fall, buffet no more with sighing
But bring my darling safely to my hand.

Reach, song, reach over remorseless breakers
Straight as a gannet skim through the sea-wind's whips,
Find out her furrows, music's unblemished makers,
Pearl the disturbing dew between her lips.

Fathomless sunbeams, sweep through the secret ranges
Coralled and shelled, waken them with your heat,
Drag up the seabed, scattering all that estranges
Till shipwrecked skulls form cobbles for her feet.

Carry my calling, echo through vaults of the ocean,
Far through the faint horizon's evening mist,
On, till the restless violence of this potion
Stills urging sleeplessness like bodies kissed.

WOMANHOOD

Womanhood washed and warm
Delays before her image in the glass
Held by her form;
Deaf to the storm
That rifts and stabs the full clouds as they pass;
Only aware of wonder in the air
Feeling her breasts unbounded and her body bare.

Come, my spring dawn, with sunbreak in your eyes,
Bud freshly blown, flower that no frosts destroy,
Beauty incarnate in her own surprise
And made a woman in a night of joy,

Division yields to dewfall when we play,
Discords resolve on music of your kiss;
Your petals turn and open to my day
And all the storms of life are lost in this.

UNHEARD THE WINDS BLOW

The thorn on the briar
  Hangs fresh after rain.
If love light so seldom
  It comes not again.

Curled close like a child
  Asleep after play,
Like eyebright in meadow
  At close of the day.

No sound but her breathing
  Breaking the calm,
Still as a baby
  At breast in my arm.

Unheeding beside me,
  Unheard the winds blow
As peacefully sleeping
  As starlight on snow.

BELLS

for Edmund

The dog-rose and the wayside poppy tell
The traveller the path they know so well.
They wave and catch his eye as if to say
'We'll stroll with you a measure of the way,
No matter though our stems dig in the ground,
Our scent and colour distance will confound;
And while the sun stipples this lazy brook
We'll loiter on the air to tease a backward look.'

Bells ring across the meadows, and the boys
Spill out of school with scrambling whoops of noise,
Scampering, scuffling, heads held under arms,
Barking up dogs across the distant farms.
June becomes jeopardy for fish and tree.
A boy's stick scythes the hedge with artistry,
The unmarked poppy and the dog-rose sprawl—
And boy and traveller some happiness recall.

THE STATUES

Bless the baby by your side!
Though the child's not yet conceived
In my dream it was perceived,
Etched out in the future's mist
Just as though a calling bell
Told a lonely boat 'All's well!'
Silver-clear across a bay,
It startled me before the day
To reassure with that strong voice
One does not question or resist.
Bless the baby by your side!
So clear a scene could not have lied.

In your lips I saw a song
Which at first I could not read—
Recondition was my need,
Yet such scholarship was wrong
For the words were simply said,
'Lay you down your milky head,
Tuck your hands inside the shawl
And may darkness never fall
On that world behind those lights
That bless my days and wake my nights.
Sleep you in your innocence,
Your gull-soft cheeks my recompense.'

Dark had just begun to lift
Yet the trees were not awake
Nor had day done more than break.
Spiders slept in dripping webs
Draped across damp window-sills,
Yet beyond the Cumnor hills
The clarity of dream remained.
The more I looked the more engrained
It grew upon my waking mind:
Two shaped rocks left as the sea ebbs—
A slender woman's sleeping form,
A watcher waiting in the dawn.

30th September 1966

121

CAROL FOR TWO BOYS' VOICES

The wet nose of the donkey
    The wet warmth of your breast—
But what strange shadow leans over
    My strawy nest?

Young farmhands come to bless my sweet
    With freshness from the field.
Like butterflies that wake too soon
    Your eyelids yield.

The roofbeams bear the winter
    Of all the wilding world;
I see them, and the shepherds—
    But what strange scurry swirled?

Your father scrapes snow from the door
    As politicians shed
Wonders I do not understand
    About our bed.

Mother, the lamb is crying
    We both of us need milk—
Who is that last that brushes us
    With midnight silk?

We cannot understand, my babe,
    These strange foreshadowings.
Now all have left, come take my milk;
    Sleep, while your mother sings:

Lullaby, lily-lullay,
Hold my finger in your palm
Tight now all the world is still.
Stay you safe from cold and harm
As within your father's arm
Sleeps the lamb brought from the hill.

SONNET

Two strangers came and sidled in my door
After you left, two I could not recall,
And being so preoccupied before
I had not anything to say at all;
No, I was dumb. On that first afternoon
You tilted up the skylight of my dark
As one might say 'Come, what a musty room!'
And force a window to reveal a park
Undreamed before. Moss-grown in blinkered light,
Vision defunct, my curdled milk of thought
Pounded to butter by a girl's delight,
Innocence teaching what no study taught.
    Your spring despoiled my common winter sense
    And peace and joy took up their residence.

JET PASTORAL

Have you the courage of your heart to sail beyond the
    sun?
Up, higher, through billowing cloud-banks, poised where
    the swallow-dive's begun,
Into the golden, cloudless blue, long earth-shadows lost
    for ever
Where crystal buckets draw up the sky, spilling your
    heart in their dance together
               And dazzling spreads
               On fleecy beds
While we wing out a world beyond the West?

Have you the daring, careless joy that strides beyond the
    sky?
Where angels picking buttercups strip old-man's-beard
    from God-on-high?
And wheeling planets wavering stand till twisted on by
    your startling hand
And the zodiac's crumpled and tossed aside in a wanton
    game of laughing pride
               Till we tread a world
               Where the dawn-streak's hurled
And sheep's wool yawns to pander eternity?

Sunlight plays ducks and drakes with the waves on Santa
    Barbara bay,
The sailing boats balloon the wind in mock Armada play;
The palms crowd like late-flowering dowagers huddled
    within their coats
And over all the green-rich hills life like a giant gloats
Birdsong content and motionless, relaxed beyond all
    care—
Lord of the edge of fecund earth, enticed by Eden's air:
Even so Cabrillo must have felt sighting this haven mile,
Storm-tossed Odysseus himself, lost on Calypso's isle.

Now the Pacific lies ahead
  One half the globe is ours,
Gentle Japan unfolds her head
Welcoming as a bridal bed
  To down-descending powers.

Another continent beyond
  The guessing side of thought
We two like eagles' brood will dare,
Like willow-pattern birds we'll share
  Music untold, untaught,

And if as now brief parting must
  Tear one flesh in two,
The hail of surging engines drown
  Communication's due,
And soaring uplift separate
  The Old World from the New,

Then, leaving far behind the roar,
When silence wakens all around
And starlight dances on your door,
Listen beyond the softest sound
And hear far off certain and sure
The linking willow-song once more,
The ancient willow-song's profound
Flight-haunting poignance wafted to the ground:

Break, sky, with all the splendour of your art,
For she has all my hope, and all my heart.

WEST COAST BLUES

I've tried so many women since I left you,
I've tried so many ways to ease my mind;
I've left my bed to drift through San Diego,
But everything I do I always find

The cold hands of the clock drag oh so slowly
Dead conversations stifle out the day
And nobody's body answers like your body
Nothing can light me up the way you say

'I love you' when you wake up in the morning
A naked lily crumpled in a sheet
'I love you' when your lips hang moist and open—
All I can think of in this rain-washed street

As I drag the boulevards of San Diego
Or wander round the San Francisco Bay
Draining down screwdrivers in topless Broadway
Through Go-Go Mardi Gras I hear you say

'I love you' to the man who lies beside you
Or strokes your hair beside the rhythm band
'I love you' to the man who fills my absence
Hangs up your dress and takes you by the hand.

I've strayed down Sunset Strip to watch the mountains
When it's just not worth while to go to bed;
Within an hour the motel's serving breakfast.
All I can think of are the words you said

The night before I left for San Diego
The night I held your wildness in my arms
The night you showed me all the ways to love you
And paralysed my heart from others' charms.

I've worn away my voice with too much smoking
I've worn away my heels with wasting time
Anaesthetized my brain with all-night drinking
But, Wild Delight, all's dust until you're mine.

126

EAST COAST CALYPSO

Kennedy Airport's bright and gay
Pink floodlight fountains make it look like day
Everybody's rich and kissing and plush
But down on the waterfront—hush! hush! hush!
New York, New York, slice of life,
When you taste it take a fork and knife.
Central Park's a peculiar place
And violence smiles with a virgin's face.

Empire State Building's very tall
They say that it sways in a rainy squall;
Janitor tells me since he began
'Fifteen fellas ha' jumped to a man.'
New York, New York . . .

Busy Manhattan's very neat,
Gardens and ice-rink along the street;
Down in the subway out of sight
No spitting's allowed while the dagos fight.
New York, New York . . .

Teachers in Harlem after dark
Never look round when they hear a bark.
Keep to the sidewalk away from the wall!
Or your wife won't recognize you at all.
New York, New York . . .

Greenwich Village is full of charm
Fashion and Painting walk arm in arm,
Your Father's Moustache draws nostalgic tears—
But how did that news-vendor lose his ears?
New York, New York . . .

Sunday last I paid my way
All up the line to Pelham Bay,
Walked in the sunshine to something draped,
A Bronx kid sobbing that she's been raped.
    New York, New York . . .

Taxi driver, he talks to me,
Says that he'll take me for a fee
Down to the Chase Manhattan Bank;
The back seat's soiled where a junkie stank.
    New York, New York . . .

Romantic skyline, Long Island Sound,
Atlantic Ocean, they're all around;
Mightiest city crowned by the sun
Where squirrels and human blood both run.

    New York, New York, slice of life
    When you taste it take a fork and knife.
    Central Park's a peculiar place
    And violence smiles with a virgin's face.

FONDLING FAREWELL

Fondling farewell, have done with dalliance,
Urgent and young, you need far more than me.
Splendour and fame must claim their recompense
And wide ambitions have their larger sea—
    Those gentle hours that you and I have known
    Fade into thoughts that linger when alone.

Go on your way, soft hands, the world is yours,
Geography encircle with a flight
Till lands that lie beneath, nations' applause,
Dazzle acclaim and take my sole delight.
    High star of fortune, sail where you are sent:
    Fondling farewell, but farewell, too, content.

I SAW A SHINING LADY

I saw a shining lady stand
In fields I could not recognize.
Caught unawares in a strange land
I stared at where her path would rise
    Across a nettled wilderness
    Shadowing ruin's emptiness.

I saw her walk on crumbling rocks
(How near to heaven I could not gauge)
But softening her barefoot shocks
Five-petalled meadow-saxifrage
    Wove yellow buttons and long stems,
    Like buttercups beside the Thames.

The red herb-Robert twined a bridge
With celandine and town-hall-clocks
Across the hard, uneven ridge
That marked decay of walls and locks,
    Roof, windows, bricks turned back to loam
    That constituted once a home.

And all my heart was filled with light
To see how she was safely held,
The stones themselves stirred with delight
And tears behind my eyelids welled.
    But when they cleared once more I found
    The Oxford traffic all around.

PAX BRITANNICA

We are the heirs of a lordly people
  Suckled on Empire's blood and wine,
Masters over mosque and steeple,
  Ambitious as angels, greedy as swine.
We are the children born to inherit
  Far dominions of this isle,
Conceived in strength and bred on merit—
  Why do our fathers make us smile?

We are the heirs of that great endeavour
  That stretched and opened up the globe,
Yet choose to disinherit pleasure
  Based on crimson gown and robe.
Rifles can no more secure us,
  Gold and trade soon ebb away;
We wonder how they could endure us
  On the road to Mandalay.

What if no longer the bugles call us
  Over white headlands, far from home?
What if our ships no more enthrall us
  Circled by jets in the shrinking foam?
What if unbounded confidence ripens
  Equally rich in tropic or snows
For us no longer? Rather, a stronger
  Hesitancy of compassion grows?

The splendour of the pageant passes,
  We watch it like a fairy-tale,
And ask the groom who cleans the brasses
  Why his stubbled cheeks look pale.
The might of Rome filled all their dreaming:
  Stripped of power we turn to Greece.
Almost too late to staunch the streaming
  We pray to learn the arts of peace.

131

THRENOS

R. F. K. (i)

The bluest sky of public claims,
Meridian of man's renown,
Casts longer shadows than it names
And strikes its honours down.

What though a vision stir the blood
Driving on to redefine
Those changing shapes half understood
Glimpsed on the edge of time?

A burning restlessness of joy,
Compulsion to wrest what's to come
Into a silver-gold alloy,
Taps the ear's inner drum.

The lounging quiet of a world
Calcined by an envious creed
Watches where morning's hope is pearled
And bullets home the deed.

1968

WREATH

R. F. K. (ii)

Even so, the legacy of bitterness,
Even so the great attempt turned quite astray.
Dusk of dawn and breaking evening streak the day.
The flowers are gathered by the light-touch frost
And those who comfort the weak
And cherish those who mourn,
Winter sunlight brief upon their eyes,
Lose consolation in their hopelessness.

So, all his faith disabled,
So many aspirations unrealized,
Even moments of glory grief, swiftly
Extinguished, flare bright, to expire;
Delight and warmth sucked by death's cold desire.
Moistened, glazed eyes
No more surprise
Dawn spreading his quickening flood across the earth.

He bore our sorrows
Promising new tomorrows
Pledging his own vitality as creed
In folly of hope
Knowing our need for even transient trust.
Blessèd are those whose searching finds despair,
Truly they care.
Blessèd the tender eagle in the sun.
Blessèd his broken carcass now the day is done.

DAUGHTERS

Firm, tiny flame asleep upon my pillow,
Your infant hands half-clenched beside your ears,
Spiders-webs brushed, and forehead clean as dawn,
    Sleep tightly on among my books.
        These early years
Shared by us three high in these college rooms—
        The oak fast-closed,
Your doll's house near and toys spread all around—
Will give you courage when flat day's steel grip
        Seems unopposed
And danger masquerades on a green lawn.
        May what's here born
        In our security
        Breed a profound
        Curious certainty
That you are safe beyond all that consumes.

Yes, you are loved beyond the leap of thought;
In my poor way protected from worst harms.
Sister shows sister masteries untaught
Till scattered hours lie strewn from dancing palms—
        Quarrelling, laughing looks,
        Grotesque, mind-toppling tales,
        Each taking turn as cooks,
Making wolf-shadows as the log-fire fails,
And if, in riding on my back, one slip,
Or I mistake, the other's quick to follow
Protect, warn, scold. Two girls: a lark, a swallow.
I watch you grow as seasons turn the years
And coming adolescence eyes my tears.

WITH GEORGIE
ON THE RAMPARTS OF JERUSALEM

aged nine

Among the trees where Jesus wept
At night we two have walked,
On stones where his grey donkey stepped
We've climbed, and sat and talked;

And high over the Golden Gate
Looked down and watched the sun
Set, till the stars showed it was late
As often He had done.

Under King Herod's massive tower
Within the citadel
We've seen the Sultan's turret flower
With dreams, and light, and bell;

And dusty slopes of Bethlehem
Have shared their shrines with us;
Alleys of Old Jerusalem
Spilled shops and smells and fuss.

Small daughter, on these sun-drenched walls
So many hands have piled
I bless you where Christ's life-time calls,
My darling firstborn child.

FOR LUCY

aged four

Spontaneous protector,
Fierce guard against the world,
Unerring lie-detector,
Whose life has scarce unfurled,

Warm certainty of duty
Is your unquestioned art;
And such transparent beauty
Dances your father's heart.

30th May 1972

SPARROWS

Do you know what I heard today?
That when Jesus was five years old
He ran out with his brothers to play
On a tow-path, and sat down to mould
Out of mud tiny sparrows whose looks
Would have startled a nun from her books.

But a schoolmaster passing that way
Intent on behaviour and rules
Knocked and asked for St. Joseph, to say
Manual work was reserved for the schools.
Sabbath-breaker, this boy in his boots,
With his jam-jar of minnows and newts.

Joseph came to the river-side
Where his son in the puddles shone bright
And squatted beside him, and sighed.
Jesus clapped his small hands with delight:
'Fly away, little birds, high and sing,
Freely dance in the skies with your King.'

THE IMPERIOUS ONES

The imperious ones—Picasso, Bacon, Moore,
Lifted above themselves by certainty,
Exhilarating self-belief so sure
That objects bend to personality,
Proud God-usurpers, dam the darting stream,
Moulding out strength from leaves of daily life,
With X-ray vision of a killer-beam
Burning fresh outlines with a surgeon's knife.
What self-renewing confidence you have!
Renaissance emperors from a broken past.
What arrow of daring there in all you gave
For us who stumble now the gate is fast!
    Humbled, I praise; yet turn, I must confess,
    To Beckett's truth and Blunden's gentleness.

REMEMBRANCE DAY

This boy with bugle in the poppied ranks
Learns nothing from a grief for bright eyes gouged,
And softness lopped between the iron furrows
Of field artillery and reef of mines.
Our wry self-brutalizing, blest as brave,
Exults like jackal laughter at a tomb:
Survivors too astute to smear a grave
We maim our sons with half-forgetfulness.
Details disturb, and no biography
Will tell the wounds this claw chose to increase.
Honours perturb, then soften into slime
Too bland for war, too hideous for peace.
    Yet still we factory our foul pretence
    And dice for war, and call it self-defence.

JUTTA

Junges Mädchen, ganz geschwinde
Unser Herz fängt Feuer.
Tanzt mit mir und dann entschwindet.
Trotzdem ist sie mir teuer,
Aber es lockt sie ein Neuer.

ELYSIUM

Loveliest of ladies, though I have no cloak
Inset with stars to spread beneath your feet,
Zealous for your delight, I here invoke
An age long past to make your joy complete.
Begun to pleasure your great counterpart,
Eliza (loved, like you, by all who gazed),
This view of human bondage dressed with art
Holds in its leaves all that mankind has praised.
Beauty reflected in Sir Walter's eyes
Under the summer sun of Shakespeare's day
Retreating hails God's courtier of surprise—
The Richard who now crowns our Queen of Play.
O eloquent and just and mighty Death!
Neglect for once your kiss of such sweet breath.

Inscribed in a copy of the first edition of Sir Walter Raleigh's *History
of the World*, and given to Elizabeth Burton on her fortieth birthday (27.2.72) in
Budapest. The second acrostic, being the italic letters joined, forms a birthday balloon.

IN HUNGARY

Wayward, and reckless of a world of cares,
I walked the Danube's waves in Budapest
Lifted by thoughts that when all else despairs
Love will create its own ecstatic zest.
Your laughing presence, though a thousand miles
Over the seas far off, made Beauty grey—
Under that arc of artificial smiles
Music herself curled up and could not play.
And as the gilded youth of the élite
Ransacked Gomorrah masquing on their fears,
Revelling in orgies clumsily discreet,
Your tender absence opened up my tears,
    Moulding till mirrors ringed around the dawn
    Even as I wrote this emblem of your scorn.

from
Emblems

EPILOGUE

Beneath this scalp within this skin a skull
Out of which peer two globes that clutch the light.
A dropped jaw parts two lips and nostril holes
Rake in the pollen of a July night.

Red bones that clasp a book pull white in sinews.
Nails protrude to gather up the dust.
The valve-fed engine thrums its tambourine
To galvanize a vagrant's wanderlust.

Home, home immortal breakers urge;
Grey mountains open the piper's note:
Dusk brings the darkness, embers mark the end—
Yet what contortion leaps the thrush's throat?

from
Troat

SONNET

Imagination's huge, informing strength
Raised with a thought; and with a word endowed
Into the quality, and feel, and length
Of anything I choose out from the crowd.
I am this elm, from frailest stalk to root;
Pervade, and thicken through warm sap to bark;
Creak the wind's strain, press out in rings that shoot
Bud-surging thrusts, while trembling limbs are stark.
I am an old man staring at the coals,
Seeking sensations while the brain runs rife;
Staring through eyes that swoop on beasts in holes;
Inhabit each last strangled cry for life.
Companion thoughts; protean, unconfined.
The spawning cancers of a dying mind.

from
Lumen

BRIGHT APRICOT

Bright apricot, kissed by the sun
And bulrush blest,
Lulled by the ripples of still yielding springs
Stretch out, my sweet
All is discreet
Here, where the easy strength of summer's heat
Leaf-lifts a shade
Of dappled willow branches I have made
Through which your skin, caressed, unharmed, may drink
The glory of the world until it sink.

Then, as dusk curls
His shimmering smoke-light round the apple-trees
And plucks each stem with darkness from its bough,
Then come with me
Warm in anticipation's tensity
Where only windowed moonlight's eye can pry
Upon such secrecies
Disclosed in flower-filled summer's stroking breeze
As make night fall
And our soft bird his breathing song of bridal call.

from
Lying Figures

AUBADE

Hush! Who is that disturbs my leaden rest
    Startling the lark?
Who makes me let the night winds feel my breast
    Calling from whispered danger of this garden?
Are you foolhardy? Reckless of all . . . Hark!
    He moves in the next room: there'll be no
      pardon.
Ah Love, since love has lit through miles and darkness to
    you,
Warm me within your naked bed that I may woo you.

My firm request you should not seek me here
    You disobey!
Your beauty overwhelmed numb caution's fear;
    Give me the penalty such wrong incurs,
Prison me in your arms, condemn to stay
    Now I am in and not a hedgehog stirs.
Ah sweet unwise, so strong to take your own possession,
Gentle me till the furthest star spills our confession.

Tenderest safety ends, the East grows light,
    Dress and depart;
Dally no more, but vanish with the night,
    Stay not to risk the terrors of the dawn,
Ring not a harebell, though you've wrung my heart,
    Nor break the melting cobwebs on the lawn.
Ah that I could sleep out all time till our next meeting;
For joy, though crown of all, is transitory, fleeting.

LYRIC

Come my little tiny child
    There's nothing now to fear,
And though outside the wind is wild
    Your warm content is here.

THE WRENCH OF BIRTH

The wrench of birth. Two bodies, puffed marshmallows
Pressed into crying, still slimed from the womb.
A sky shrunk to a pillow wet with grief,
An earth contracted to a spasmed room.

Call on the angel of your agony!
Naked the nettles touch among her fears.
Torn by a tumour nursed in tightened skin
She begs the cruel mercy of the shears.

Let me reach out across the darkening lake!
Oh little children, yet the briefest while
We live to grieve our bearers, till the rake
Claws out our wisdom with our bloody tears.

from
Killing Time

THE UNIVERSE SPINS ON A SHAFT OF LIGHT

The universe spins on a shaft of light
    Whose name is love.
Flowers of the meadows folded up all night
    Spread for high strength above
Them, warming out their secrets till
Displayed for all to see each world's a daffodil.

Full-blown with morning, laughing to the sky
    With puckered lips
They kiss sun's mastery to catch his eye.
    No night-jar trips
Among the undergrowth between the stars,
For violets and primrose chain the bars.

I took a prism, dazzled as a king,
    And held it up.
Light shattered into all the flowers of spring.
    Kingcup
And stalked marsh-marigold, its spendthrift son,
Transfigured all around till night and day were one.

What vision have I seen? Flowers wheel like suns
    In daisy-chains of dance
Round daffodils, whose green-gold laughter stuns
    To ignorance
My day-dull thoughts. Then suddenly the clue
To all was clear. That source of light is you.

CLOSE, CLOSE TIGHT BUDS

Close, close tight buds now parting ends the day,
      Laughter must cease
Colours fade and withering winter come—
      Yet say, even as you droop
And nod down to the roots from which you grow,
      The shadows know
Even as they stretch their fingers on the lawn
No parting's loss when lovers long for dawn.

Seal up, sweet lids, the trembling of damp eyes
      And glistening cheeks;
Strength is a beauty only known in grief:
      Like men at war
Who find true comradeship in cruelty
      And bravery
Even as they mourn the very friends they kill,
So may this night of parting bind us still.

SLEEP, MY LITTLE ONE. HUSH!

Sleep, my little one. Hush!
The guns chatter all night,
Their flames are lively.
Sleep, my little one,
Soon you'll grow up and play with them.
Hush, it is nothing, my little love,
Close your ears, sleep, sleep,
It's nothing, just life.

from
Meeting Ends

PROLOGUE

A sunshaft strikes the steeple by my room,
Flares the high cock that crowns created day,
Strips the moon's nakedness from her star-cage
Lordly demanding more than lovers' play,
Rouses a million sleepers from their gloom
And burns its image on this frozen stage.

Now the dead miser's hoard is flung across
Those blackfrost fingertips of darkest grey.
Magnificence of dawn, fresh in its birth,
Opens exulting eyelights in a spray
Of tints refracted like a woman's loss
Of graveyard chastity in glowing mirth.

Ice wisps its crystals over brown and white
Till footsteps fill again in brittle black.
Grass tufts in the snow's mud, lichen on bark
Curl green on brown against the wind's attack
Now lightfresh keen, claiming each stalactite
Of frozen immobility from dark,

Till broken architectural schemes of ice
Hung up in stillness by the moon's delay
Bow their reluctant torsos to the spell
Of bluehigh soft prebirdsong's proud display,
While here below the crosswinds stir and slice
The freshening fur beneath the beetle's shell.

But higher than the not yet risen lark
Three wise men from the west reach for the moon
And far in space look back on the good earth
Unlikely in vast silence to cocoon
Life on its surface, which may be as stark
As this dead rock of sand and crusty dearth

Now reached. And yet Earth looks so small, so
    blue,
So lovely an oasis, that a spark
Of heaven might once have touched some one-
    celled life:
But mastodon, or grain of wheat, or shark—
Gross fantasy; and for man to be true?
Reason rejects such lunacy run rife.

EPILOGUE

But in the blue of that light space oasis
The predatory sea-wolf's granite jaws
Crunch on a morning crab whose shell is slashed
To tongue the living meat from out torn claws
Till anarchy is gorged, and Scottish faces
Peer at the netted fury hauled and gaffed,

While far beneath the dreams of northern keels
Men crawl the ocean's yet-unrifled bed
Sheeted in gloom to ravage, kill, and farm,
To understand the uninterpreted
Half of this mighty globe, till it reveals
What teeming recompense can keep man warm.

Yet at my feet a snowdrop breaks moon's winter,
Its secret yellow trussed up in green gauze
Traced round and rimmed with white, and all
    enfolded
By three white lips that shield it out of doors,
Weighing down like a bell from a sheathed splinter
This surge of life the icy dust has moulded.

SUMMER WALKED IN LAST WEEK

Summer walked in last week
With daisies on her fingers, and a shawl
Of fresh-lost music scattered down her form.
    I rubbed my eyes
But still the sunbeams danced. Yes, I recall
When light-pinned stars beyond the storm
    Blessed their surprise
On windflowers waving by a river's brink,
    Yet should I think
That there was no mistake — this was for me?
Within whose skull old wary spiders prey
And for whose throat a grey bird whets its beak?
    Sure, it can't be
Unless the world's grown young and lost dismay,
And tears can laugh, and softest touch will stay.

THE NOTES LIE STILLED

The notes lie stilled as dusk folds down the fields.
Sleep, my sweet lady, here, where all art lies;
Summer's enchantment all its glory yields
And airy wonder fills your closing eyes.

Rest, while the masters of our waking joys
Rule over us and stretch the oceans' clutch:
The silent stars play havoc with our toys
But we have kingdoms that they cannot touch.

Lighten your dreams beyond the reach of thought,
Skill's farthest limits are within these arms;
And in the circle that our warmth has bought
Your safety's milk lies soft between my palms.

Lucca Quartet

for Lorraine

CAMAIORE

Peace in the afternoon
  Sparkling eyes;
Sunbeams are rafters
  Stillness flies:
Wildwood contentment
  On hillside and path
Pinetree and olive
  Watch the hearth.

Farmyards of Tuscany
  Cupped in hills
Move in the shadows that
  Brightness fills.
Steep paths hesitate
  Stepping in green;
Dark wine for cover
  And lover's screen.

A baby is sleeping
  Through distant bells,
A bride in the valley sings.
  Smoke curls
From a weather-worn building
  Tiled in sun
Like your cheeks when happiness
  Is done.

Calm and elation
  Create this room.
One child paints flowers
  The other soon
Will call from the dusty track
  'Wake up! Let's start!'
Those years of your sadness
  Bred sweetness of heart.

May wings stretch over you,
  Spring touch your vein,
Loveliness lighten
  To childhood again,
Falling hair fasten
  Love to your breast
By Florentine scentfall
  Caressed.

CHORIAMBICS

We are still wide-eyed awake. Come, shall we tread
        out on the bare-foot paths
With the cool wind on our face? Yes, while no clothes
        bother and night is ours.
We have both whispered so late eagerness sings,
        blood is alert. Next door
Two soft brushed children asleep, safe in shared warmth,
        laid like sardines, secure
From all hobgoblins and fears, terrors and ticks,
        giants and walking trees
That bedtime stories have spun, read with a last
        bloodcurdling tender squeeze.
All the still valley's asleep. Cold in neat graves,
        lit by electric coils,
The long-past dead of the farms, cemetery snug,
        glimmer their distant light,
While the stream washes, the breeze clouds out the moon.
        Beauty, star of my sight,
Kiss me once more. Let us stay here
        now, while the first bird calls.
In our flight far from the grey desolate days—
        acres of years misspent—
We've discovered the best. Here let us rest,
        living complete content.

CANZONE

Here sits the chess-set, silenced *in flagrante*
When your self-mocking anger
Mated checked love and challenged concentration.
Here sultry postcards, Carracci's Bacchante
In tongue-tied exultation
And the Urbino Venus caught in languor,
Mother shocked stiff, scolding enough to hang her.
Here is the Elvis record, our reveille,
Lucy's sweet welcome crayoned for your breakfast—
They knew we always wake last
Dressing themselves and skipping down the valley.
Here are the trophies of our climbing zest
But what is goodness if we lack the best?

You have returned to face the storm-wind's music
With heightened trepidation,
Branches of marriage falling in cold greeting.
What inner certainty drove you to choose it
A week from our first meeting
Turning all trials to wild exhilaration?
Spontaneous love's the father of creation.
When envy creeps up through our doors and shutters
Damning our sins, preaching anathemata
In hate of spring's cantata
Laughingly lived and sung past sneers and mutters,
Let us ignore caution's catastrophe
And breed proud children in shared ecstasy.

MADRIGAL

'Will she ring, will she come?' Children, what can I say?
I will wait as I've waited, indoors this spring-fresh day.
You must delight in the open, run, risk and dare
All the adventures of playtime. I will stay here.

'Does she love, was she happy, wandering the world as
   ours?'
Children, sunshine is brief in a lifetime of showers.
Our magic carpet was perfectest joy Fate can weave—
If now unravelled, little ones, we must not grieve.

Over the mountains, bird-song in Tuscany
Still haunts the leaf-time, heightening memory.
Over the years such love will come your way.
Outside now, darlings. Please don't look. Just turn away.

SONNET I

Is it a wonder that I love you so
When everything about you is a greeting?
In spite of your forced frown at our fresh meeting
Your body, hands, eyes, cheeks, delight and glow.
Is it so strange I simply do not care
What is the cost, what transitory grief
Must be endured, though surgery is brief,
If your decisiveness cuts swift and clear?
Is it a crime to know one's inner mind
And tell it to you, without hesitation,
Openly, trusting, knowing masturbation,
Guilt, subterfuge, despair are all you'll find
    If you decide to take the cautious way,
    Choose second-rate and waste the dawning day?

SONNET II

Was it mere chance that brought the mating hare
Almost to touching distance as you stood
Still as a tree beside the sunlit wood
Downwind of him, your beagle nowhere near?
Were the white streaks along his whiskered cheeks
Furrows, too, caused by solitary tears?
Did his loose lope, his absence of all fears
Delight you? All his muddy scattering freaks?
Didn't you feel a happy naturalness
When his doe crossed the harrow to his side?
That all our Spring is blest, and has not died—
That deep love triumphs over danger's stress?
    Wasn't this vision in your saddest hours
    An emblem, darling, of what might be ours?

Lucca Quartet, 11–14 April 1975

Lyrics, Public and Private

FOR JENNY BROWNLOW

Outside your cottage window, summer's joy,
Jenny, enfolds young happiness in green,
Endows on all whom love seeks to destroy
Nurture, till healing friendship makes serene.
No one I know has your perceptive grace,
Your understanding sympathy of heart,
Brightness of sight to speed the sunbeams' race,
Richness of thought to make the angels start.
Outside and all around, you shed the peace
Which happy marriage radiates on all
Near by, till saddest thoughts find some release
Like sunshine on a hidden waterfall.
    O Jenny, you have taught the birds to sing
    While shadowed happiness is on the wing.

TO AN ARTIST

for Josephine Skinner

When goat-foot gods and naked woodnymphs peer
        Once more
    Dancing a new world's spring
And our sad doubts are dusted all away,
Then, when old buzzing love is sure
        And has no sting
And old age smells as sweet as apples stored,
    Silenus and his sons
Will search about to find one sunbeam more
    And hesitate their dance
Till sweet Jo join them on that harvest floor.

COLLEGE ROOMS

Lucy in the great armchair
With her loose and golden hair
Writes a poem late at night:
Only stars give any light,
All the world is shadow-land
While her firmly moving hand
Builds on the page her dream of dreams,
Imagination's silk that seems
Clothing for the saddest mind,
A shelter where all life is kind.

CHRISTMAS DAY CAROL FOR A CHILD

Christmas is a time of sadness
    Overwhelmed by joy,
When gentle sanity calms madness,
    Bringing a baby boy
Shivering and shut-eyed in rough straw
    Helpless and pink and weak
Whose playthings are the stars, his door
    Lit by a comet's streak.

Today perhaps another world,
    Planet light-years away,
Welcomes the same Creator, curled
    In bed more strange than hay,
Born afresh a tiny thing
    Suited to that far star
Where they now sing their new-come king
    Transformed as we too are.

And one day every furthest speck
    Unseen in outer space,
Every space-mariner on deck,
    Lonely and out of place,
Will hear a gong ring through the dark
    To say that all is done—
Jesus has planted all his park,
    The universe is one.

So bring in holly, light the fires,
    For he has other sheep
And other folds as well as ours,
    And we must vigil keep
To welcome them. Yes, here they are
    We've passed them every day;
No stranger from a distant star
    But the poor we turned away.

25th December 1977

179

RICHARD, QUINQUAGENARIAN,

If distant ages look back on our years
Curious to know the myths by which we live—
How our imagination dried our tears
As Empire's actions grew contemplative—
Richard, they'll thank you that retreat from power
Diademed into all the arts that flower.

Acknowledged round Earth's little ocean ball
Now seen against its lighting-chart of space
Deified with your lady, loved by all
Eurydice herself returns with grace.
Love is life's drama, poetry its land:
Interpret still until all understand

Zeitgeist and zest crystallize in the part
Applauding History calls you to share
Because you two make life a work of art
Endowing myth with joy, and joy with care.
    Take up the tale, embody our ideals
    Happy the night that rings these wedding peals.

WHEN, ON THE FARTHER SHORE IN TIME TO COME

When, on the farther shore in time to come
(Be it far off!), our gentle Frank arrives
There will be waiting both a Zulu drum
And British bugle, calling up past lives.
Gathered in musket lines and bandaged ranks
To welcome him who blessed their memory
Back here on earth, both sides will offer thanks
For *The Red Soldier* by Frank Emery.
Zulu and South Wales Borderer now are friends,
For animosities of long ago
Pale into gratitude as each intends
To thank their wise historian from below.
    Each, black and white, will come in turn to tell
    Him, none but he re-lived their hell.

FOR ROBERT AND ELIZABETH BURCHFIELD

5th November 1976

E vening will soon be here, and all the air
A live with echoes from fresh wedding bells
R ung for an Oxford globe-embracing pair
W hose starry joy the evening light retells.
B ring on fresh candles as they go their way
U pon their journey, let the champagne spill!
R iches of happiness be theirs today
C rowned in a night sky lit by fireworks, till
H alf Europe wonders why the sky's ablaze,
F abulous in the darkness. We will say
I n simple truth, in blessing and in praise,
E lizabeth our loved one's wed today.
L ove her. Turn night to light. All ringing's rung,
D ear prince of words and master of our tongue.

181

INSCRIPTION

In a copy of Edmund Blunden's *Near and Far*,
presented to Robert and Elizabeth Burchfield

Robert, you knew and loved him as did I;
Shared his wry jokes, sweetened late Oxford days
In his last years, when ghosts from Picardy
Came crowding in. He gave you highest praise:
And he, I know, would be the last to hide
His joy, and mine, in blessing of your bride.

AMERICAN HOTEL, AMSTERDAM

for Nico Rupke

Chinese art-deco lamps, and trams here are
Suspended in the 'thirties, while my friend
Reads a Dutch time-table with his cigar.

James Joyce is writing, trying to pretend
He does not see us, clamping bishop's gaiters
Around his mind, determined to offend,

While we become anachronistic gapers,
Leisured. The cavernous management provide
Discreetly lit the thoughtful newspapers.

Two girls with legs, one dark, one blonde, outside
Compel our eyes across the Leidseplein
Past the Schouwburg until they sit beside

Fern-plants that come between us. We are vain:
Call 'Ober!' Ask him to convey a pun
In verse and wait till they respond again.

Their answer is in prose, though they are none.
We watched them rise with the approaching sun.

3rd January 1977

FOR KOINONIA

She shone from a sea of faces
A sun-danced wave of the bay,
Others in orderly places,
Her beauty in disarray,
Their brows in concentration,
Hers clear as a bell at night,
Her skin as high as elation,
Her cheeks my entire delight.

I see a dream around you,
You slip half in, half out.
I reach to help surround you
Above, between, about,
With threads of golden lacework
Woven in snowflake stars
Until the dream grows tangible
And you heal my face of scars.

Ah, fresh as the milk of morning
When the half-awake clouds are piled
Welcomed as love is dawning,
Woman no longer a child;
Death is to me no stranger
Although I wish he were:
I'll lay you in a manger
And cradle you with fur.

24th March 1977

A SONG FOR KOINONIA

Come, say no more. There is no more to say.
Long fields are shadowed now with end of play
And laughter's thoughts diminish with the day.

Flecked eggs no longer warm the sitting rooks
And busy terms with tutors, lovers, books,
Pass into history through backward looks.

Though all has nearly gone, this will remain,
This thought, this memory to ease my pain;
That you have miracled the world's disdain.

And in you Beauty finds she will not change
Whatever cruel vicissitudes derange
Or doctors, husbands, parents may arrange.

Your goodness is incarnate in that glow
Of gentleness that I lost long ago
And never thought to find again below.

So may all years and countries be to you
Blessings as tender as each life that's new
With silent promise in the morning dew.

SONNET FOR KOINONIA

I went to Binsey but you were not there,
Although the sun still warmed unshadowed lawns.
I watched the white doves strut around the chair
And wasps spill beer and chutney in their swarms.
Restless I walked where river weeds had grown,
Preoccupied with thoughts of you away
In a far country, unattached, alone—
My music with no instrument to play.
I left September bundled up in bales
And climbed the library where every dusk
I'd find you stooped among your travellers' tales
High up in Bodley, like an owl in musk.
    Binsey or Bodley, by our books or stream,
    Delight's pale shadow is my cherished gleam.

from
A Conception of Love

WHAT IS IT IN YOUR WALK, YOUR FACE, YOUR EYES

What is it in your walk, your face, your eyes,
So startles, lingering in the memory?
The way you talk, your grace, immortalize
These passing moments with their melody.
Time spent with you is heightened, clearer-etched
Like Evesham valley sunlit after rain,
And no ambition for you seems far-fetched
When we have met, and know we shall again.
Your voice hangs in the air, though notes have
        passed,
Like pollen filling summer nights with scent
That stirs the heart and wakes the unsurpassed
Joy that your gentle company has lent.
With you love, beauty, memory distil
A pearl of rarest truth time cannot kill.

LET ME CONFESS THAT IN MY SECRET MIND

Let me confess that in my secret mind
The claw of bitterness has gripped a hold
On sad occasion, and quite undermined
The quiet hope that kept me from the cold.
Let me confess, too, that I have no cause
For cavilling, and should throw care away.
Hasn't the sun brought laughter out of doors
And spread a primrose carpet for the May?
Haven't I to my touch new leaves in bud
And music everywhere in bush and tree?
Doesn't the very air breathe likelihood
Of love united, flown across the sea?
Let me confess I have no cause for weeping;
And ask, for absolution, your safe-keeping.

MAY THE HEALING ANGEL TOUCH

May the healing angel touch
Your swansdown body with so much
Pressure as will heal and cure
With true health that will endure
As love endures; for body should enjoy
So richly that no illness can destroy.

SEE! THE LIGHT FAILS ON THE
DARK WATER THERE

See! The light fails on the dark water there.
Put sprigs of secret myrtle in my hair
    For bridal love.
The railway sounds more clear now, comforting,
With the late birds' brisk twitters echoing
    In the still air.
The darkening grass folds up the daisies' heads,
And blackening trees brush children to their beds.

Tie up our toys, for we must face the world.
Please would you put down, where that hedgehog's
    curled,
    This saucer of milk?
He's my new friend. The sycamore's winged fruit
Will soon be spinning the moth's parachute.
    I'll share your life.
My sleeping breasts will rise for you alone.
Your lips sealed up, my garden is your own.

DUET

(He) Look back, look back! *(She)* Not so. *(He)* Why
  won't you stay?
(She) What's here to stay for? *(He)* All my life is
  yours.
All that's to come. *(She)* The time has passed for play,
I must away. *(He)* I'll turn to none but whores!
    (She) Take whom you will. *(He)* Can you not
      even grieve?
    (She) We met, we've tried, we've grown apart,
    must leave.

(He) Let me try once more! *(She)* Flowering time is
  brief,
Girls cannot linger, waiting love's return.
(He) We can look back and build on more than
  grief!
(She) Our freshness has departed, and concern
    For you as much as me makes me depart.
    (He) I'll win you back! *(She)* Fool! Do not
    break your heart.

(He) What will you do? *(She)* The world has men
  enough.
(He) And yet you said adulteries must cease!
(She) They must. *(He)* How then? What will you do
  for love?
(She) I'll braid my hair, live cross-legged from the
  knees.
    (He) Where will you go? *(She)* Where you must
    never seek there:
    I'll live the College Master's new housekeeper.

EPILOGUE

Oxford now in history lies
Held a moment in moist eyes
Blinded by what's left behind.
All neglected learning's joys,
All the ageless girls and boys,
To transparent gold refined.

Laughter, lovers, beauty, youth,
Nightly arguments on Truth
No more all together found,
For relationships will fade
And the outer world invade
Till our friends are underground.

Memory alone can hold
In its myth-creating gold
Echoed music's treasured sound.
Yet one hope beyond the last
Moment can yet still hold fast:
This new love that we have found.

from
Light Shadows

THE DEATH OF SENECA

You sent the order Seneca must die,
And his fine ashes now hang in the air
Brightening the twilight; and his wife, Paulina,
Loving her husband, also cut her veins,
But she is safe under your guard's arrest,
And she will live. Seneca did not weep,
Or criticize the Emperor he taught,
But finding death too slow for his quick mind,
Longing to leap into eternal light
And leave this night of aching flesh behind,
He took some hemlock from a hiding-place
And made libation, both to Socrates,
And Jupiter who sets all prisoners free.
Then in warm water his lean body wept
Until the steam, rising to saddened heaven,
Carried his life beyond the morning star.

Morning Vespers

for Rosalind

I

Beloved friend, your faith has come to mean
More to me now than I could once have dreamed.
Your personality, wild, yet serene,
Untamed, yet gentle, deeper than had seemed
At first in my dull stumbling through the wood
Of this dark world, has grown into my thoughts,
Filled out my days, refreshed with wholesome food
Where I before had drunk the sailors' ports.
Your love, unscathed, has risked through brothel streets,
Searching me out between sheets of despair;
Borne with my shadow-screams in wintry heats;
Stepped between fighting razors with your care.
   In youth and beauty you bring all, to give;
   And loving life, you teach me how to live.

25th July 1978

II

Blessed woman, wayward child,
   May no harm come near you,
You who've shared your tender years,
   Growing pains and fears, too,
Trusting me in everything,
   Knowing I'll protect
Whether life caress or sting
   And all else be wrecked.

Wayward woman, blessed child,
   Have no further fears.
Though winds of doubt turn inside out
   I wipe away your tears
Until uncertainty's dispelled,
   And where a confused girl rebelled
Our strong love strengthens, and is held
   In arms now reconciled.

23rd October 1979

III

You came to me at nineteen
  And took my heart away
And wrote a loving letter
  For three years every day.
You made my children love you
  And shared our private joys
And lying on our pillow
  Whispered you'd breed me boys.

You taught me so to trust you
  That I could face old age
And that you'd never falter
  But all my needs assuage.
When the full horror hits you
  Of what this is you do
You will come home to welcome,
  And I will marry you.

7th November 1979

IV

Sadness salt-deeper than the sea
Stings the raw weeks till your touch heal
And unabated misery
Turns in the gut like swallowed steel.

What crime can so deserve such pain?
What hatred take such keen delight
That each day's haemorrhaged again
And shouted prayers deface the night?

My sockets have no more to give.
Familiar agony returns
Increasing till the will to live
Diminishes in napalm burns.

Each imposition we inflict
On others at our own expense
Strikes back its cursing interdict
Till savage love claims precedence,

And we, poor mortals that we are,
Cringe as we feel our faults return,
Knowing full well sold vows must scar
Another, yet resent our turn.

There is no balm in selfishness,
Evil cannot be self-contained
But grows and spreads till less and less
Can claims of peace be entertained,

And where we thought a little wrong,
A slight withdrawal, soon would heal,
We find dead roots grown far too strong
Till joy's impossible to feel.

Before self-loathing overcome
The perjured with the perjurer's sin,
Bless, while our hearts can still be one,
And let love win.

5th November 1979

V

Eight winter weeks have dragged their weariness
Across our lives since last we lay so warm
Enfolded in each other's gentleness
And petalled splendour of your naked form;
And yet two hundred weeks of shared delight,
Of growth lived to the height of ecstasy,
Loved by two children, blessed by God's own might
In never-failing shared intensity,
Have been our envied, legendary days.
The orchard apples rot upon their boughs.
Both lives hang stagnant till our wayward ways
Return and join, fulfilled in love's own vows.
   Never were two so well prepared to share
   One life of love than this tuned Oxford pair.

Binsey
16th December 1979

VI

The world turned upside-down has made us pause
And gather up the wonder of our cause
To give us breathing, meditation space.
Yet sorrow's wisdom holds us by the hand,
Teaches me treasure more your unique grace
Poured out like Spring's pulse on the waiting land.
Your early twenties can no more return,
And yet, distilled in perpetuity,
Our love continues, deepens, builds upon
Such single-minded pure intensity
Until, two thousand past, we both look back—
Our children's children dazzling as the sun—
In joy. Sweet Rose, though these last days seem black
In this new decade we two will be one.

30th December 1979

VII

These Left Bank streets so effortlessly ours
And Paris walks so wanly desolate
In days without you full of empty hours
Mirror bright windows where we would create
New myths and hopes, turned dust upon the tongue,
Unbearable. Each footstep, gallery,
Clothes-shop and monument's a memory wrung
With your continual presence, agony
Bleaker than bodily pain, harsher than grief
To counter, lemon in the eye of pride,
Impossible to heal or find relief
From gut-torn longing for you as my bride,
   And life without your love a worthless waste
   When all our deepest vows are so defaced.

4th January 1980

VIII

When I was eight I took a burning-glass
No larger than a pebble sliced in half
And concentrated all the summer's sun
Ten thousand times its strength upon one spot,
Glowing, until the edge of some dry leaf
Fanned into smouldering till sparks caught fire.
Such energy, I knew, could also blast
Spider's leg, ant, or beetle. This strange thought
Widened the ring of light and softened strength,
Touching the small boy to humility.
Much later, now, I find this God-like power
Hides in a grown man's all-embracing love,
Rides over all vicissitudes to leap,
Clutch, pierce, and focus two lives in one flame.

7th January 1980

IX

Your hand in mine, we watched a sunbeam strike
The dancing dust in Lavenham's old church
Soaring and falling all the scented, sung
Evensong in a joy-shaft on our love
Till, setting as we fulfilled down the hill
Back to The Swan, to live what we had felt,
The dusk enfolded in its soft embrace,
While the last marigold transformed your face,
Killing all trace of any sorrows past,
Tracking a stairway from your smile to heaven.
Now darkness falls indeed, and no beams dance.
Hands reach, but only find dust on your heart.
Proud tenderness must wait with patient faith
And watching through the long hours of each night.

26th January 1980

X

The iron law of right and wrong has claimed
Its penalty for sacred love blasphemed
As we both knew it would, exactly timed.
Maimed, I survive. The other man you loved,
Your father, the sad sacrifice, commits,
Refined, his soul to beauty of our best.
His death on your Damascus road can bring
Good out of evil, if humility
Like Paul's accepts rebuke as holy food
Stinging to heal and turn round into God.
Years back we two were set apart. A ring
Would be our aspiration's longed delight,
Now a command. Wrath's awe is understood.
Kingdom or chaos is your lifelong choice.

11th May 1980

XI

The deepest sadness is when one heart turns
Away, first having willed, with blessing's self
Over the years the other's love, and learns
To prey upon those joys it nourished most.
Now evil spreads like cancer through your days,
And nine-months' love-denial has destroyed
The Paradise where now a donkey brays
Grand in its scorched-earth landscape of complaint.
Yet those whom you loved most still love you now,
Child of reversed emotions, near despair.
Love is most proved when joy's most cherished vow
Wildly disintegrates, yet faith holds on.
    Our four-year home is nine-months tempest-tossed.
    Rose, let not dearest loveliness be lost.

27th June 1980

Entr'acte

FOR PENNY AND ROBIN HODGKINSON

13th September 1980

The looking-glass of long divided years
Dissolves into a single wonderland
Of harmony like music of the spheres
Heard only when such spirits understand
True love, as Bride and Bridegroom here, who meet
Never to part, vowing love to suffice
In matrimony, holy and complete—
The crown of life and glimpse of Paradise.
A silent crystal in a noisy world
Shining in purity of selflessness
Is such a moment, when two lives are pearled
In one, as Earth and Heaven conjoin to bless
  The highest aspiration that we know:
  The love of God reflected here below.

LYRIC

for Susie

We race the skies to meet, while all the globe's
Cities and wildernesses wait our steps.
Whether we wink in academic robes,
Or kiss in Paris over street-side crêpes,
Or laugh with ancient Egypt in Turin,
Or walk the walls of Petra high on gin,
Kingdoms are gambled by us high above
Like swallows chaosing in gleeful love.

15th February 1980

Spring Harvest

I

May the snow upon your lids
Sleep till melted into dreams,
And those dreams ease what forbids
Answered loving, which redeems
Everything through Heaven and Earth,
Flowering bodies brought to birth.

In my eyes you see you are
All that wildest hopes can wish.
Milk spilt from the furthest star
On a beam that wise men kiss
Bursts into a prism's range
Of glory that can never change.

Even so your altering eyes
Never less than full of love
Burn the sacrifice where dies
All save rarest joy, above
All mankind sets dear apart—
The purest moments of my heart.

II

Sometimes a summer's day begins in mist
And light's expectancy unwraps the trees
Raising the grass to green from amethyst
And whitening soft bird-song melodies.
Heart-lifting certainty the gleam will spread
Irradiates each nerve and every leaf
Across day's blue dominion when the shed
Darkness dissolves and splendour conquers grief.
Opening eyes see all creation waits.
Richness arrives, outlined in early dawn.
Everywhere certainty anticipates
Youth's wild fulfilment as our love is born.
    On comes our day, our lifetime of delight
    Unhurt and marvellous as morning light.

III

When you disclose your beauties to the air
In tenderness of wide-blown innocence,
Like April roses when great thunder's near—
Lightning above us waking more intense
Your milk-flushed skin, firm in its stripped pretence,
Or overhead the wrath of mountains bless
Us with cataclysmic violence
Making thick rain applaud our wild excess—
All nature hesitates in spread suspense
Revelling in the life-force on the briar
Rose-blushed and open in magnificence.
Your elemental thrust of air and fire
    Meeting in storm and lightning will create
    Earth-born new life that leaps through Heaven's gate.

IV

Music is in your blood and in my heart
As we compose our lifetime's masterpiece.
You have the gift, the high, creative art,
Growing in strength, through ecstasy to peace,
Of making sacramental each soft day;
Drawing your finest flowers from my dull weeds;
Bringing out shapes and patterns as you play
Love's complex symphony of words and deeds:
Even to make our most fantastic dreams,
Spontaneous hopes and proud, high-darting fires
Swell into sunrise as your beauty's beams
Yield into fact our fantasies' desires.
    Oh Sarah, you bring joy to birth, and prove
    Under your modesty, creating love.

V

Morning and new-born star so frolicsome,
You are the dayspring from which pure light starts.
Diamonds and opals set in gold become
A true-love's knot, shaped in a pair of hearts.
Ravishing are your breasts, your sea-soft skin,
Lovely as lightning are your answering eyes.
Innocent wantonnesses, silk beams, spin
New threads to brim our endless ecstasies.
Gone are the sighs that greyed a setting sun.
Strength is our tenderness no night can smother.
As we lie here we are two worlds made one,
Risen to irradiate and complete the other.
Ah, my sole joy, and joy of all my soul,
Hold in your hands and heart a man made whole.

VI

Mastery lightens the sky as Venice rises
Yellow-gold, knowing, complete on the waves of her
    sickle
Lagoon, with San Marco, her palaces, squares and
    surprises
Over the Grand Canal, where fresh blood can still trickle
Viewed from the stone-humped Rialto. Now, this clear
    morning,
Enchantment touches endearment with nakedness
    sleeping—
Innocence fallen from Heaven, our world freshly dawning
Scattering darkness for ever in mutual safe-keeping,
Wonder incarnate, more precious than all this proud city
Imagined it flaunted when Genoa, broken, defeated,
Trashed here the boast of her wealth. Serenissima's pity
Holds back no gift from her children whose prayers have
    entreated
Marriage of city and ocean, bridegroom caressed.
Etch your light, Venice, to bless the soft head on my
    breast.

VII

Out of a grey sky came your wind of spring
Under the buds, stirring birth with sun's breath,
Royally proving on excitement's wing
Love is larger than life, stronger than death,
Opulent without material needs,
Victorious because it cannot lose,
Enriching and ennobling all the creeds
Ignorant man constructs but cannot use.
Spring joy, this glorious summer-scented world
Of ours, of dappled light's security
Flooding our daily leaves, driving them, swirled,
Galvanized into stripped fecundity
 Of soul and body, is the highest reach
 Devotion knows, for each is all to each.

Selections from
Moving Reflections

SECOND PROLOGUE (JOHN)

Those who reject love find love rejects them,
The full, rich tide thins, swamps, ebbs out, till sharp
Granites of lifelong pain rock pride's ripped craft
As human diminishes, and jaundice swells
Leaning on righteous crutches: 'Pity me! Pity me!'
To stagger self-condemned, weep in a mirror
Half-lit, rather than say 'Yes! I was wrong!'
And turn. Such claw flesh from their cheeks and beg,
Cringe for affection, kill where they would curl,
Needle heroin into their mothers' breasts
And jaunt on egg-shell, tip-toe in despair,
Still boasting to ignoring crowds 'I'm right!'
The artery severed and their life-force dead
To evoke from hell this fundamental law—
Our dance of darkness shows light loves.

TIBERIUS (i)

From here, Capri, my garden island fortress—
Fragrant in spring's first Mediterranean light,
Sweet with the scent of cypress, mist, and vines,
Blossom and pines and myrtle pure as snow
(Though Venus' flower) and all migrating birds
That wing the cliffs one thousand feet below
From Africa, weaving swift threads of silk,
Darting each grotto cool and dark as a shell,
Stroking the waves, to soar and settle high,
Here, on their long flight, till with dawnbreak song
They leave for Europe and the farthest North;
Though not this redbreast—look! pricking my
    finger
He hops and trusts in full throat, Rome's, no doubt,
Bringing the news Sejanus' neck is cut,
Pruned by my gardening letters to the senate:
I, master of the world, Tiberius Caesar,
Princeps, Pontifex Maximus, Administrator
(My proudest title, I disdain all others
Save Poet), from this high Tarpeian rock,
I rule the world bequeathed me by Augustus,
One time my guardian, stepfather, and god,
Augustus Caesar, dead for fifteen years;
And I myself now threescore years and ten,
In self-imposed, protective exile, searching
For peace, restless and waiting.
He used to sleep with his hands on his eyes
In this same room, his summer residence,
Mine all year round. Across the bruise-soft sea
Beneath those heights of Cumae there's the cave
Aeneas found in which the foaming-mouthed
Sibyl Deiphobe answered his prayer
Foretelling wars, and Tiber red with blood,
Days come and gone. And yet strange opal words
Sung by our gravest singer, who taught me
When I was young, Virgil: he said that Time,

Pregnant, was bringing to birth a new Apollo,
And all past centuries of hated wars
Will cease, the night of horror end with dawn.
Creation dances in expectancy.
Lion and ox will play in peace; foxgloves,
Smiling acanthus, ivy, Egyptian lilies,
Will shape themselves his petal-pillowed cradle.
Where is this god, forecast when I was born?

TIBERIUS (ii)

Alone. Capri.

These cliffs, these softest breezes on my cheeks,
I love them as they soothe my ruffled bed
By lamplight as dawn breaks. I cannot sleep
While the long letter to the Senate lies
Unfinished on my table. It is easy,
Too easy, to destroy; but to create
As our great architect of empire did,
Augustus, is a miracle. Men's hearts
Are savage. However spurious their loves,
At least their hatreds can be counted on.
Am I transformed, deranged by total power,
As men say? No. Saddened. My solitude
They misconstrue debauchery. At my age!
The dawn voice of the sea! (*Writing*) 'Herewith
    I banish
Actors from Rome; they fornicate the women
And stir up riots.' Paulina has been fooled,
Her chastity violated? A lovesick youth?
What's this? 'Bribed priests enticed her overnight
Into the Temple of Isis? Decius Mundus
Dressed in a dog's head, calling himself Anubis,
Enjoyed her all night long? Her husband's stained?'
Those old priests shall be crucified. Their temple
Demolished. Their wooden statue of Isis thrown

Into the Tiber. Mundus is banished. *(Writes)* At
   least
He loved. Oh Rome, Rome, Rome!
Hectic and sprawling megalopolis;
I am as stern with myself as with you.
No, I will not accept your fawning gifts
Of flattery; and senators, why, why
Abase yourselves, offer me empty titles:
'The Father of us all'; a shrine—such baubles?
Should I, who broke the greatest nations, and
Declined so many Triumphs in my youth,
Bend to the foolish crown of a suburban
Parade in my old age? The fact, not dress,
Of power preoccupies my darkening mind.
The weight and care of service to the state,
The Empire, and not least the provinces,
You should share with me. But you cringe; defer
To me, and go home early. Read this, loud,
To the full Senate: 'Every Senator
Must work full hours. No one may be condemned
To death without a ten-day interim,
So I can sanction or reprieve.' We must
Conserve, continue, and build this great work
Of world peace. Compromise, commodity,
Those twin gold eagles of the Roman State
Are not enough. *(Writing)* 'If I knew what to write
To you at this time, or what not to write,
Senators, may heaven plunge me in
Worse ruin than I feel now overwhelms
Me every day . . .' *(Writes)*

THE RESURRECTION

MAGDALENE I spend my nights crying. Tears are on my cheeks
when I wake.
No one can comfort us now.
Jerusalem, built on two hills, surrounded with honey
walls,
You have become a criminal; your dress drags in
the dirt.
In the souk little children sigh standing in open
places.
Does it mean nothing to you who pass by? Has
there ever been anguish like mine?
Our too-much-loved city degraded; our music and
laughter silenced.
Even the sun is eclipsed. An earthquake has
shattered the Temple.
Was this the perfection of cities, the joy of the
whole earth?
Now women abort on benches and there is no one
to help.
The cats and dogs will be eaten. The sucking child's
tongue turns black.
We drink our own water: there is nothing to fill
our breasts.
My dancing is lost to grief, my long hair matted
with sorrow.
Oh God, oh God, come and help me! The joy of
my heart has died.
(To audience) Does it matter so little to you that
our city of peace has committed
Consciously, with false law, smeared with the cant
of religion,
The murder of Goodness on earth?
And now they have taken my Lord, and I don't
know where they have put him.
Wasn't his life enough for your cruelty? Couldn't
you leave us his corpse, just his body?

CHRIST *has entered behind her, and she becomes aware of him.*

You, sir, if you have seen any soldiers or priests
    while gardening,
Taking away our friend, tell me, Where have they
    laid him?

CHRIST   Mary.

MAGDALENE *(Turning to him)* Rabbuni! *(Drops on knees about to clasp his feet)*

CHRIST   You may not touch me now, because I have not yet
    ascended;
But go and tell the others that I am ascending to
        My Father
        And your Father,
        My God
        And your God. *(Exit)*

MAGDALENE *(Pause) I have seen him! (Runs off)*

JOHN (i)

This cool shade of the cave, this burning desert,
This Roman world so slow to learn the truth,
The way, the life . . . How can I with rough pens
And only parchment skins to write it down
Complete some memories of all he said
In that brief, perfect life once shared with me
So long ago? Days spent in hot Judaea,
Samaria, and dark Jerusalem, .
City now utterly destroyed, her walls,
Her sanctuary battered down by Titus.
Now only Herod's empty towers stand:
Three monuments to Caesar's butchery.
All Jesus' closest friends are taken back
To God, save only me, last one on earth
Who shared his human thoughts and prayers;
        my Christ
With laughter, tears, and blessing on his lips;
Who skimped his meals, and would neglect his sleep.
When I am loved into eternal life
This last surviving link will be extinct—
Though only in the flesh! The Church moves on
As resurrected body of our Lord!
Now, on my hundredth birthday, I will spend
All the thin heat this body burns, to write.
'And John the Baptist said, "I am the voice
Of one that's crying in the wilderness
'Make straight the way of the Lord!' I am not fit
So much as to undo his shoelaces
Who is amongst you now. Why? I baptize
With water, but he shall baptize with fire.
Immeasurable distance separates
Pale onlooker from looked-at Light itself.
See! Now the sacrificial Lamb of God
In innocence and saddest gentleness
Lays down his life to clean the wickedness
Caused by us all in this our cruel world . . . " '

My ink's congealed. Alke! Please bring some fire
To melt it, or I'll use blood from my veins
To fix the memories omitted by
Mark, Luke, and Matthew, which will die with me
Lost, unrecorded, or in garbled fable
Tickle the ears of unbelieving smiles.
Alke! A girl, though young enough to be
My great-great-great-granddaughter, loved of God.
Burrhus and she guard me from Ephesus
In this my cave, until my days are done.

JOHN (ii)

JOHN   *(Slowly)* You think your family will Judas you?
       Alke, come here. God has decreed you shall not
       Have to endure torture. There is an island
       Shaped like a horse's head and neck; just three
       Volcanic mountains, like the Trinity.
       It's very small, and very beautiful.
       The waves around it are a sea of glass,
       And from the mountains, light divides the world
       As you look down. The walls are black, like jasper,
       The city gold, brighter than chrysolite;
       The streets are clear as pearl, and the swift stream
       Brighter than diamonds left in the sun.
       It was a penal colony of Rome,
       Then left deserted. Now, our Christian refuge.
       I have a son in God who bears my name;
       There he will honour you in his old age
       As I have done—and you must care for him
       For he, too, has a mighty book to write.

ALKE Through you I'm happy. But you seem to be
       Preparing us for days when you are gone?

JOHN   I am. My work on earth is nearly done.
Burrhus, if any part of this our Gospel
On which I have been working seems unfinished,
You, who know all my literary thoughts,
And Alke, you who know what I would write,
Complete and tidy it. Mankind still craves
For books they can think sacred. Look what Greeks
Have done to Homer—allegorized bloodshed.
The Jews, too. In my Gospel all is there
The intellect of man can wrestle with;
For guided by the Holy Spirit I
Have told his doctrine of divine compassion
Through allegories, juxtapositionings,
Statements, exempla—with severe retraint.
Yes! Even Pliny and Quintilian
Might nod in our direction. But we speak
For centuries to come. Thousands of years
From now, perhaps, some distant northern island
On the far limit wall of Empire,
Rome's farthest outpost, will repeat these words
And be brought home to Christ. Burrhus, tell me
The news you bring of our Ignatius.

IGNATIUS CONDEMNED

IGNATIUS   Yes, Polycarp. Ten of those savage leopards—
I mean ten Roman soldiers—are my gaolers.

POLYCARP   Ignatius, how can you endure their taunts,
Their casual bullying, their sadism?

IGNATIUS   They try to make me live up to my name
And watch me lose my temper. It is hard.
One of our golden-tongued brothers in Christ
Called me 'A soul seething with divine eros',
And they have jeered about it ever since.
But, gentle Polycarp, we must put up
With everything for God's sake; so that he
May also endure us! I am the least
Of all the flock, the latest to the fold,
Least worthy, and deserve all this, and more.
Thank you for comforting me in your city
Here. I have often longed to be with you
In Smyrna. Now I am. My chains are jewels
Whose preciousness has brought us face to face.

POLYCARP   *(Kissing* IGNATIUS's *chains)*
Father of God, our bishop of Antioch:
I do not have your learning, nor your age,
Experience, or sad predicament . . .

IGNATIUS   Sad? Yes! But never plead for my release.
I am a convict. You, thank God, are free.
Yet this entanglement in Satan's power
Among the Roman eagles has led me
Into the deep thoughts of our Jesus Christ.
Even as I say this, oh! the Devil laughs
To hear me boast in spiritual pride.
I have become afraid to hear the comfort
Of those who tell me I shall win a crown

228

Of martyrdom. Not that I fear to die,
But compliments become a scourge to me
Because they fan my impetuous ambition,
And at the very moment I can see
Armies of angels battlementing heaven
And mighty Peter bending down his hand
To lift me up to walk among the ranks
That part and glitter in gold martyrs' crowns
Above the principalities of God
I choke and struggle and am thrust to hell
Snatched at the height of joy. So bear with me.
The truest consolation you can give
Is gentleness in prayer for my pride.

POLYCARP What of the friends who plead for your release?

IGNATIUS This journey I am taking has begun
Well. I am prisoner of Jesus Christ,
Even as Paul, and many blessèd saints
Before me lead the way. What I fear most
Is not the cry the circling crowd applaud
In Rome, but generosity of friends
Who would prevent me dying like my Lord;
For I shall never have so clear a chance
To leap to God again.

POLYCARP Your roots of faith are firm, and bear rich fruit
For our Lord Jesus Christ. We came with nothing
Into this world, and neither can we carry
Anything with us, save a perfect end,
The consummation of a life of prayer.
Stand firm in your great passionate content;
Steadfast, immovable. And when you reach
The farther shore beyond the storm-wind's strength
Pray for us here below.

IGNATIUS   I will.

229

THE DEATH OF POLYCARP

ALKE He was condemned to burn before the crowds,
With twelve, I think, from Philadelphia
Who also stood firm and would not curse Christ.
Orthodox Jews in Smyrna hate us more
Than most, because our teaching supersedes
The Pentateuch. They rushed, with others too,
Collecting wood and kindling from the baths
And workshops. He took off his bloodstained clothes
Down to his waist; tried to undo his shoes,
But was too weak—and stood inside the circle,
His back against the stake. They locked the irons
Around him, but when nails were to be hammered
Into his limbs, he said 'You have no need
To nail me. God, who helps us to endure
The fire, will also help me to remain
Here at the stake unmoved.' And so they spared
    him;
Tied him instead. Yes, like some noble ram
From a great flock offered in sacrifice.
He prayed—I could not hear now—then the
    flames
Blazed up. But God was kind. The hasty
    faggots
Encircling him drew air up in the centre
And no flames burned him. Like a vaulted chamber,
Or a ship's sail filled out with wind, the fire
Curved round. It was a miracle. A sweet
Scent rose up from the woodsmoke. Flames died
    down
And he was still unharmed. They called the man
Employed to give the coup de grâce to beasts
In the arena, the confector, who
Had not gone home yet though his work was done.
Grumbling, he came out with his new-cleaned knife
And stabbed our perfect martyr Polycarp.
The blood poured down extinguishing what little
Fire was left. (Weeps)

JOHN   You need tell me no more.

ALKE   I'm sorry. But the hardest part for me
          Was that my brother made impossible
          Our burial of his body; with a sneer
          That Polycarp might rise as well, and we
          Would worship Polycarp instead of Christ.

BURRHUS   What then?

ALKE   They burned him, and we have his
              bones.

JOHN   He wins the crown of immortality.
          Ignatius, too. May the Almighty God
          And Saviour of our souls, with all the saints
          Rejoice above.

War

BEIRUT, APRIL 1983

Muezzin at dawn, three-thirty, jerks me awake:
Metallic, interminable. Overhead,
So low I see its pilot from my bed,
A lone, dark bomber crawls north for a break.
    Black-eyed for sleep, and hot,
I doze. Cock-crow. One double rifle-shot:
Put—put. Again. No more. Dogs bark, cringe, trot,
As I look out across the burning tyres
As muezzin ceases, and the night expires.

Why do they bring me to the battlefields?
Haven't I spent enough time close to death?
Haven't we thrown away that shibboleth,
'The public needs to know'? Here, nothing shields;
    This is not breakfast food,
But unbelievable at home. How could
I tell the sickening smell of widowhood
Without a gross betrayal of all trust?
How can we look on war without disgust?

If the bomb-thrower saw the patient's bed
In which the victim of his violence lies,
Surely some slight remorse would fill his eyes;
Or do our hatreds strike compassion dead?
    The surgeon's finger drums.
Here every psychopath in Europe comes
To claim his scalp from bloodlust in torn slums.
Each loved life gone had so much more to give.
Man plays at God to find he cannot live.

The 'plane has gone before the sonic boom
Announces its arrival, and the bomb
Has split the high-rise sea-side hotel from
Itself, where head-masked snipers have nest room
    To pigeon-shoot at will
Pedestrians. I have seen how they kill.
A girl of nine was skipping down the hill
Dancing the sun. One shot and she was still.
Her scream will never leave my window-sill.

This place was Paradise on earth. Now great
Metal containers stacked like sugar-cubes
Form half-safe sprint-ways in between the feuds,
Down to the ships, up to the hotel gate.
    High children snipe, for sweets.
Yet, to this desolation of burned streets,
This anguished cry: 'What is it that defeats
Evil like ours?' we must respond, with pain,
To bring to Lebanon its peace again.

KING'S COLLEGE CHAPEL, CAMBRIDGE

The held cascade of vaulting stone unites
Two roses in the Tudor white and red.
See! Every soaring window's highest lights
Demand, undimmed, that no more blood be shed.
The spacious grandeur of this house of God,
Dreamed by a saint, heals internecine blows:
Where seventh Henry's filial steps have trod
Beaufort portcullis joins the Tudor rose.
True, the next Henry set his feet astride
The airy music to enlarge our eyes,
Carved sad initials on his screen, and died,
But we are heirs of all that enterprise;
Still reconciled by men of lifted view.
Lord, let not England fall again in two.

Thanksgiving

RUBAIYAT

Ah, Georgie; you and I have travelled far
To where the crescent meets the morning star;
From citadel of David to the Sphinx,
From Baalbek's sands to Karnak's Amon-Ra;

And when the Master of our Fates decides
To show the glory that our frail flesh hides,
One grove, one river in that Paradise,
Will be our mirage where the Bedouin rides.

LETTER TO LUCY

Though I am far, and you remain behind,
Untouched bloom of my heart, breeze stilled to gold,
Gentle in beauty, excellent in mind,
Our sixteen years' companionship will hold
Up the bright edifice of adult years
Ahead. The garden of your loving play
Will flower in rich profusion free of fears,
Happy and fertile as a field in May.

And I, high in the sky, lifted and fresh
(England's green quilt seems very far away),
Exult that you, my poetry made flesh,
Will live beyond my petty judgement-day
To find new worlds, of faith, of lust to live,
Strong in a love that far outlasts the tomb,
Forged through your childhood, now your own to give
Your man, your children, to the crack of doom.

What stormy night did you come into the world?
What brush with stillness preluded your breath?
What marvel, heartbeat, through that storm that hurled
Its thunder round the sky and promised death!
Out of the darkness comes a flickering light,
A tiny daughter hesitates to live—
Life falters; wins. My gratitude that night
Spreads down the years, compelling me to give

You blessing from above the Memphis clouds
Touching the sun, like Icarus, in blue
Carefree, entire in happiness that crowds
In on me as I wing home back to you.
Soon we shall be in Rembrandt's home, perhaps;
See where Anne Frank's life-innocence was lost—
Our million joys have covered many maps.
Ah, may you never more be tempest-tost.

April 1984

EPITHALAMIUM

for Penelope

This girl all in white is my crystal of light
Kissed by heaven to earth in a dancing gift
Of a bride in her freshness, whom youth and love lift,
With two sunbeams for bridesmaids, their father's delight.

I have married my bride in a ring of green fields
Round a church on a hill where all nature's her dress,
While below the bright lake reflects heaven's caress
With a leap of the organ and towered bells' peals.

The sheep stray up close leaving wool on the hedges,
Their gifts for her future; town friends are our guests.
Here the wheat, there the barley, wave from the lanes'
    edges,
And house-martins flash bringing song from their nests.

The rice will be scattered, her blossom will glow
As new garland, and sheaf, and the berry-bright trees,
And the laughter of friends, and the families grow;
And our spring-wind will dance on the grandparents'
    knees.

> They say that on the bridal-day
>   (Unless I am mistaken)
> The music of the spheres is heard
>   As holiest vows are taken
> (And I can hear them now. Can you?)
>   And all the plants awaken
> And stay awake the whole night through
>   Till morning sheets are shaken.

The pink-turned-blue forget-me-not
  With no stalks on its leaves;
The sun-gold lady's bedstraw
  (No sting nor prickle leaves);
Love-in-a-mist sky-blue and white,
  Soft maidenhair and comfrey—
These will delight my girl tonight
  With heartsease in the country.

Later today we'll be scattered away,
  But something is altered for good:
Here death is defeated by life-giving love,
  And light conquers dark, as it should.
May our joy and our thanks race the blood in your
    flanks
  For, from where you have come, far and wide,
You have honoured and blessed of all moments the
    best:
  When a man takes his girl as his bride.

Envoy

One rhyming verse for each day of the week
With sixteen quatrain lines for daylight's hours,
Then twenty-four lines follow to complete
Night's clockface while the bridal dark is ours.
Posy of song, live on to sweeten years
To come, when winter's shears
Harvest the loveliness about us now—
Take the pink rosebuds from the bridesmaids' cheeks,
And the white garland from my darling's brow.

Blagdon
2nd July 1983

HOTEL PALUMBO, RAVELLO

Pasquale, on your leafy mountainside
Where gentleness and quiet touch the vines
With summer's vintage ripening in pride,
Your loving welcome courteously shines.

Accept our gratitude, wise friend and guide.
May all the blessings of these ochre towers
That ring their bells as evening takes the hours
Be yours; and may these bright and soft-voiced flowers
Recall your poet and his new-wed bride.

July 1983

INSCRIBED IN A COPY OF *MOVING REFLECTIONS*

Were old Tiberius once more to leave
The noise and dust of Rome for southern peace
He would not choose Capri. No. He would lease
Palazzo Palumbo for his reprieve.

July 1983

LOVE'S COUNTERPOINT

The cliffs divide our song.
Subject and counter-subject prick their art
  Like a bee on a girl's breast
    Shocking and strong,
We wait astonished, hoping for the best.
Yet do not grieve for newly-weds apart:
Tears wash the cheeks but cannot change the heart.

    Ah yes, it's true
Absence is gilded by first light's fresh hue
    When thoughts of you
Awake my darkness and make all things new,
And reuniting is our morning's due.
Closed eyes can see, even absence makes us one:
So pauses hold the notes resolved to unison.

                                    20th June 1984

FIRST SOUND

My everlasting springtime breeds
   A flower new-born
Through not yet ready with bold needs
   To claim its dawn
Under the sky veins of great nature's dome;
Yet the wild heartbeat has been heard at home.

Touched by daylight, I throw the sheet
   As cockcrow calls.
Quick with excitement in bare feet
   I climb down walls
Where olives thicken on their bark-damp trees,
And thank life-giving God upon my knees.

Here all around flower and leaf
   Lift with the light.
Each blade has a bright drop. Relief
   Opens my sight
To Brunelleschi's dome, half-found through mist:
A girl in beauty radiant where we kissed.

She's far across fish-heavy seas.
   Mint-scented plants
My confidantes share in day's breeze
   The wild-flowers' dance:
A stem with five white petals waves to show
Its minute fire of gold packed tight in snow.

Each olive leaf points up. Wind strikes
   Ripe, heavy pears
Through glossy leaves. That trunk with spikes
   Oranges bears.
Behind me rises the all-ripening sun
And the new moon's nine circles have begun.

This stream over Etruscan stones
  Will still be here
When the as-yet-unborn condones
  Grandchildren's cheer.
Though grey hairs come one day, yet earth will still
Praise new life won on Fiesole's hill.

25th September 1984

Index to Titles

251

Index to First Lines

252

253